DAVID P. H. JONES
MARY G. MCQUISTON

Interviewing the
Sexually Abused Child

GASKELL

© The Royal College of Psychiatrists 1988

ISBN 0 902241 23 0

Gaskell is an imprint of the Royal College of Psychiatrists,
17 Belgrave Square, London SW1

First published 1985 by The University of Colorado School of Medicine
Second edition 1986
(Edition 2 still available in the USA as No. 6 in the Kempe Centre series)

Third edition 1988
Reprinted with amendments 1989

Typeset by Dobbie Typesetting Limited, Plymouth, Devon
Printed in Britain at the Alden Press, Oxford

Contents

Acknowledgements

Many individuals, including abused and non-abused children, and professional colleagues, provided us with help and understanding in the writing of this book. We are particularly grateful to Dr Gail Goodman; her understanding of the available research on children's memory helped us in Chapter 2, although the views expressed are our own. Laurie Shapiro's comments were helpful to us in preparing the second edition. Lynn Betz did valuable research for the appendices to the first two editions, while Christa Laird helped prepare them for this third edition. Lois Robinson provided valuable secretarial assistance.

DAVID JONES
MARY MCQUISTON

Introduction

Although instances of what may now be described as child sexual abuse (CSA) were described in the book of Genesis, there was little professional concern with the sexual abuse of children until recently. Freud's case descriptions from his 'adult survivors' remain vivid, but they were superseded by his more acceptable theories of infantile sexuality and fantasy. There was a marked increase in interest about the physical abuse and neglect of children in the 1960s, and this was followed by a similar concern with sexual abuse in the 1970s and 1980s. The basis for the conclusion that a child has been physically abused remains the identification of inadequately explained injuries, while that of neglect rests upon the observation of deprived standards of parental care with consequent ill effects upon the child's normal development. Sexual abuse is significantly different from these two. Recognition of sexual abuse depends upon hearing what the child has to say, and only rarely does the recognition depend upon physical examination or findings. The child's account is of prime importance, which is why this publication has been prepared. The interview with the child is of crucial relevance to clinicians, police, and courts. We have produced this short book as a handbook for those who talk with children who may have been sexually abused.

The assessment of possible cases involving CSA has come under scrutiny in all countries where the problem of CSA is being recognised and addressed. The UK is no exception, and, at the time of preparing this third edition, we are digesting the conclusions of the Cleveland Child Abuse Inquiry (Butler-Sloss, 1988). It is clear that an assessment of possible cases of CSA must follow principles of accepted good practice already existing in the fields of child psychology, psychiatry, and child-welfare work. The interview with the child must be supplemented by enquiries into other areas of the child's life, including family life. In order to achieve an adequate assessment, the multidisciplinary approach is of primary importance, and the recommendations and practices described in this book are intended to complement, rather than substitute for, the procedures and practices of the individual professional disciplines. Furthermore, the way in which the interview with the child fits in with other parts of the multidisciplinary process of assessment in a community must be worked out on a local basis, aided by the establishing and publication of agreed procedures to be followed in response to suspicions of child abuse (Department of Health and Social Security, 1988; Bross *et al*, 1988). We hope this publication will be of value to medical practitioners, social workers, police, nurses, and others who have to talk in detail with children. We presuppose a working knowledge of child-development issues, as we regard this as a necessary basis for working professionally with children.

Why write a special publication on interviewing the sexually abused child? After all, surely sexually abused children are just the same as any other troubled children? We think that, even though the principles involved in interviewing children concerning their psychological problems may be familiar ones, there are issues peculiar to the child who has been sexually abused, which warrant a special publication. The book is organised in the following way.

In chapter 1, we describe the pressures that come to bear upon the child victim, both within the family and from the system outside. These pressures can be considered by examining how the problem presents to professionals. For example, the presentation may follow a single abusive incident or may occur after many years of intrafamilial incest. The resulting pressure on the child differs greatly between these extremes, especially as the child may be perhaps 3 or 13 years old when the abuse is disclosed. A working knowledge of these pressures helps the interviewer to appreciate how different the children are who are unified by the experience of being sexually victimised. There is a growing appreciation of the dynamics of victimisation, which has been derived from the study of victims of child abuse, spouse abuse, and other violent crimes. A knowledge of this area is a prerequisite to approaching child sexual-abuse victims, and is outlined on pages 6–8.

We conduct interviews within the context of the available research in the field. Recent developments in the fields of cognitive psychology, the memory ability in young children, the child as witness, children's 'suggestibility', language, and knowledge of sexuality are incorporated into our practice. Relevant aspects of these areas of inquiry are reviewed in chapter 2.

Chapters 3 and 4 cover the interview itself. In chapter 3, we discuss the important preliminary considerations, including the setting for the interview, the presence of parents and when and how the session can be recorded. The last section of chapter 3 is concerned with which professional should interview the child. We emphasise that although a full-scale interview is appropriate for certain situations, it is inappropriate for professionals such as paediatricians, general practitioners, or health visitors, who need a brief screening approach for everyday practice in cases where suspicion of sexual abuse arises. We have therefore outlined some suggested approaches for such a screening interview in chapter 3. In chapter 4 we deal with the full evaluative assessment interview. Finally, validation is a crucial issue both for clinicians and the courts – is the child giving a truthful account? In chapter 5, we present a clinical approach to validation.

This book does not attempt to cover all the areas relevant to interviewing sexually abused children. The reader is referred to more general texts that cover interviewing and diagnostic assessment of children to place this book's focus on sexual abuse into context (Cox & Rutter, 1985; Hill, 1985). The assessment of mental status or the psychological impact of abuse is not covered. We do not cover the entire field of abuse and neglect of children, and again refer the reader to more general texts for this (e.g. Helfer & Kempe, 1987; Mrazek & Kempe, 1981; Sgroi, 1982). Our focus is on the evaluative interview. In this third edition (UK), there have been extensive changes, but not to the fundamental orientation of the book, which is to be a guide to those who need to know if a child has or has not been sexually abused. All the sections have been updated, and some have been completely rewritten. The chapter on the interview itself has been reorganised and some new sections added.

1 The predicament of the child sexual-abuse victim

In this chapter, we describe the pressures and influences that affect the victims. This clinical understanding can help us to appreciate the predicament the victims find themselves in (Taylor, 1982), enabling us the better to understand the child whom we are interviewing.

Before the predicament of the victim is described further, we must define child sexual abuse (CSA). The most frequently quoted definition is that provided by Schechter & Roberge (1976): "the involvement of dependent, developmentally immature children and adolescents in sexual activities that they do not fully comprehend, and are unable to give informed consent to and that violate the social taboos of family roles". A shorter working definition has been provided by Fraser (1981): "the exploitation of a child for the sexual gratification of an adult". We have found these definitions to be useful pointers to the general area of concern, but lacking in specificity. We have therefore preferred to use a definition that is operational and that specifically describes the terms of reference (Oxfordshire Joint Child Protection Committee, 1987). It is based on the definitions used by Russell (1986), Finkelhor (1979), and Mrazek (1981). Our definition is long and seemingly unwieldy, because the concept of CSA embraces a wide variety of sexual activities and sexualised interactions that involve children.

> Child sexual abuse is defined as the occurrence of a sexually inappropriate act(s) involving a child, which is committed by a person who is 5 or more years older, or who, in initiating the sexual act, exploits the child in question.
> 'Inappropriate acts' include the following; acts of exposure; genital fondling – child's or adult's; penetration – oral, vaginal or anal; and rape.
> 'Exploitation' refers to the balance of power between the child and the other person, at the time the sexual activity first occurred. (*after* Russell, 1986). Thus exploitation is considered to have occurred if the activity was unwanted when first begun, and involved a misuse of conventional age, authority, or gender differentials.

In general, the "5 or more years" age gap is part of our definition. However, in children under 5 years old, all activities falling into the above categories constitute CSA. Also, in cases where a possible victim and abuser are less than 5 years apart, the situation is examined for signs of exploitation (cases of brother–sister incest are thus often included despite less than 5 years' age gap if exploitation was present at the initation of activities).

Presentation

Children may disclose the fact that they have been sexually abused at many different points in their life. It is known from community surveys that many adults have never disclosed the fact that they have been sexually abused (Finkelhor, 1979; Russell, 1986). It is probable that the majority of victims, in the past at any rate, did not tell anyone about their experience. However, we can describe some of the common presentations of the children who do tell.

People who have been sexually abused frequently delay reporting what has happened to them. All the major studies and case series consistently emphasise that delay is a major clinical feature of CSA cases (for example, see Meiselman, 1978; Finkelhor, 1979; Russell, 1986; Conte *et al*, 1987). There is less delay in reporting CSA committed by a stranger. Thus, CSA is brought to the attention of someone else besides the child and his or her abuser. This process of 'disclosure' occurs at a variable period of time after the CSA has begun. Furthermore, for some children, CSA starts in infancy, while, for other victims, abuse starts in teenage years. These variables notwithstanding, we can look at presentation both from the perspective of when the child presents and how presentation occurs.

Ounsted & Lynch (1976) first described the *Open warning* in the field of physical abuse, whereby the parents let a professional know, often in an ambiguous way, that all is not well within the home and that their child is in danger. They noted that the professional often responded by *Gaze aversion*, turning a blind eye to these and other warning signs. In sexual abuse, the situation is similar, but this time it is the child who tries to alert the world to his[1] plight. The child may make an ambiguous statement, perhaps about "another little boy I know", ascribing his own experience to this other mythical child. Similarly, younger victims may simulate cunnilingus, fellatio, or even attempt intercourse with a friend while playing; this, too, may provide an open warning to a parent or professional. Older, more verbal children, may attempt to drop small hints about their experience to a trusted friend, schoolteacher or counsellor, or to a neighbour. Adolescents may run away for no apparent reason, perhaps hoping that someone will ask them the question that they have felt burdened with for

[1]The use of feminine and masculine pronouns is interchangeable throughout this book.

a long time. All these expressions of distress may be understood as 'early' or 'open' warnings that sexual abuse is occurring to the child in question.

Children may make far more direct statements to parents, relatives, adult or child friends, or to counsellors and teachers about sexual abuse. Unfortunately, that person may or may not listen to them. Many victims report being disbelieved or even admonished for their untruthfulness when they make their first disclosure of sexual abuse. (Burgess & Holmstrom, 1975). The effect of such disbelief or inaction by a professional person may cause the victim to retain secrecy for many years. When a direct statement is made, it often occurs when the child feels comfortable; for example, during preparation for bedtime, or at bathtime. It seems that, at these times, the world feels relatively safe to the child, and perhaps also, the act of undressing facilitates talk about her own body. For example, one young child, when being bathed by a trusted parent, pointed to her genital area and said "daddy kisses my pee pee". Usually children disclose a small portion of their total experience initially, apparently in an attempt to test the adult's response before letting them know more about the assault. If they receive a positive and supportive response, they may feel safe enough to disclose more about their experience.

A change in behaviour is common when a child has been sexually abused (Conte & Berliner, 1988). In general, children tend to respond to specific stresses in a non-specific way behaviourally. This is the case in child sexual abuse, too. The most common behavioural consequences in the victims are neurotic disorders or disturbances of conduct that may be of a relatively non-specific nature. There are, in addition, some more-specific types of behaviour that occur in sexually abused children and may act as pointers to the possibility that sexual abuse is occurring (for a review, see Browne & Finkelhor, 1986). Some of these behavioural sequelae are discussed below under *Effects of child sexual abuse*.

The first presentation of sexual abuse may be a physical illness. Venereal disease in prepubescent children indicates possible sexual abuse (Neinstein *et al*, 1984). Some children present in hospital emergency rooms with physical evidence of an assault or rape (Kerns, 1981). Cantwell (1983) has shown that the examination of the vaginal opening of sexually abused girls can provide useful information as to whether there has been attempted digital or penile penetration. Frequent urinary-tract infections in girls without clear physical cause may also raise the question of child sexual abuse. Enuresis and encopresis are common accompaniments to child sexual abuse; however, studies to discover what proportion of young children with these latter problems are sexual-abuse victims have not been done yet.

Some young people present for the first time when they become pregnant (Mehta *et al*, 1979). Sometimes the adolescent becomes pregnant by her first boyfriend as a means to leave home or as a result of her promiscuity (Lukianowicz, 1972). On occasion, however the pregnancy is an incest pregnancy. Such young people guard their secrets and do not disclose that the fathers of the children are, in fact, their own fathers. At this late stage in the biography of incest victims, they have become 'participants', and incest pregancies are tangible and constant reminders of their feelings of guilt and shame.

For other children, the first presentation occurs when they cross to the other side of the fence and perpetrate the act to others. Their access to younger children may occur with peers in playgroup or school, or may occur for the first time when, as teenagers, they babysit young children. (Meiselman, 1978; Becker & Abel, 1984).

Many victims do not present until adult life, and as such appear to be overrepresented among the patients admitted to psychiatric hospitals (Gelinas, 1983), and among those attending sexual-dysfunction clinics. Additionally, incest victims are overrepresented among those who injure themselves (Simpson & Porter, 1981), attempt suicide, turn to drugs and alcohol, and who become prostitutes (James & Meyerding, 1977).

Summarising, presentation may occur at various points throughout a person's life. Delay before disclosing sexual abuse is commonplace and may be extended for many years after the event. There are five main modes of presentation:

1. through an account by the child;
2. through disturbed behaviour or changes in behaviour exhibited by the child;
3. through physical signs and symptoms;
4. through an association with other forms of maltreatment;
5. by allegations arising from parents, relatives, or other adults.

The most common mode of presentation is through the direct statement of the child (Conte *et al*, 1987). The first person whom a child normally tells is another child of the same age or thereabouts. The second commonest mode of presentation is for the child to tell a parent or trusted adult.

The effects of child sexual abuse

The predicament of the child sexual-abuse victim can also be understood by considering the behavioural effects of child victimisation in more detail. We have already noted that children respond psychologically in a non-specific way to specific stressors. However, within the field of child sexual abuse, there is the added factor that the abuse itself is not a unitary phenomenon. Children who have been assaulted by a stranger on one occasion are grouped together with children who have been the victims of incest for many years before finally disclosing their plight, and all these are described as 'child sexual-abuse victims'. In addition to the heterogeneity of the experience itself to a child, there are additional factors to be considered. For example, the extent of neglect, emotional abuse, deprivation, or even frank physical abuse, is likely to have an impact on the psychological state of the child. We also know that the extent of the child victim's involvement in pornography and 'sex ring' activity with others, appears to have an influence upon outcome (Burgess *et al*, 1984).

Most professionals who meet with child sexual-abuse victims observe the psychological sequelae of the sexual abuse in the weeks and months that follow disclosure of chronic abuse. By contrast, the psychological after-effects of the assault itself are usually only seen in those children who are the victims of a single assault by a stranger, and whose parents take them to an hospital emergency room or a rape crisis centre. The effects observed at these two points appear to be quite different. For example, the psychological after-effects of an acute assault are similar to those observed in adults following rape (Burgess & Holmstrom, 1974; Everstine & Everstine, 1983). The child shows symptoms of acute anxiety and agitation, with nightmares, night terrors, specific fears or phobias, and a fear of an attack. Guilt feelings are common, with depressed affect and sometimes a predominant feeling of helplessness. Gender and other sexual-identity problems may develop in boys who fear that they will now be homosexuals, and girls who become convinced that they are 'damaged goods' (Porter *et al*, 1982).

The effects seen during the time that abuse is repeatedly occurring are variable. As already stated, the most-common reactions are non-specific, neurotic disorders or a deterioration in the child's conduct. Thus, children may become more anxious and fearful, be unable to concentrate and attend to their school work as well as they had, and show evidence of sleep and appetite disturbance. Similarly, other children show signs of withdrawal, and may be mildly depressed with guilty thoughts and the expression of more anger than is usual for their character. Some children's conduct deteriorates and they may begin to lie about everyday events, steal, or become aggressive with their friends. Preschool children may develop temper tantrums, whereas adolescents may 'act out' in a more dramatic and obvious fashion. They may become involved in drugs, make suicide attempts, run away, or simply become beyond the control of their parents or teachers. There is an association between teenage pregnancy, anorexia nervosa, teenage prostitution, and a prior history of sexual abuse to the child.

How many children who are sexually abused and then disclose their abuse, show behavioural change in the subsequent weeks or months? Estimates and studies suggest that approximately two-thirds will show moderate or severe evidence of emotional or behavioural change of the types listed above (Conte & Berliner, 1988). In the other one-third of children, there is either no, or else mild, psychological disturbance; however, we do not yet have the long-term follow-up studies to enable us to know how children in this latter group fare when they grow older.

A significant number of children develop a post-traumatic stress disorder (American Psychiatric Association, 1980) after they have been sexually exploited (Conte & Berliner, 1988). This disorder consists of recollection phenomena, a numbed emotional responsiveness, and signs and symptoms suggestive of hyperawareness and anxiety, with a tendency for everyday occurrences to act as reminders of the old trauma, resulting in an unpleasant flood of panic feelings.

School failure may result from an increase in their anxiety and agitation that develops after repeated assaults. A sudden deterioration in performance may occur. However, it is important to note that some children may respond in a paradoxical way in school and become overachievers in their drive to overcome their personal secret. The first-class student who is a good athlete – surely he cannot be a child sexual-abuse victim? It is known that such an adaptation to repeated stress can occur (Rutter, 1985), and many case histories attest to it.

The follow-up studies that have been conducted indicate that those children who were victimised at the youngest age and involved for the longest period of time, and where the severity of the abuse was greatest, are likely to show more severe psychological sequelae (Browne & Finkelhor, 1986). However, it is probable that other factors, such as parental emotional unavailability, neglect, physical abuse, and involvement in pornography, play a very important role when one considers the psychological effects upon a child. In addition, the effect of the intervention of the helping professions along with the legal response (see *The effect of the system* below) may have a significant contribution to the overall impact.

Victim psychology

The psychological adaptation of the child sexual-abuse victim in response to continued abuse is a key factor in appreciating the current psychological status of the child to be interviewed (Summit, 1983). The developmental process of becoming a victim is a complex one. When we are evaluating a child shortly after disclosure, it is relatively easy to forget the long process of adaptation that all family members will have gone through before the current time. The chemistry within the family necessary for abuse to occur starts early, long before the child is actually sexually misused. In intrafamilial sexual abuse, various family patterns are possible. Sometimes the child and future abuser are emotionally close to each other. Gradually the abuser sexualises the contact between them (grooming). In other respects the abuser may be relatively emotionally available, yet paradoxically misusing the child. In other situations the abuser's relationship with the child may be hostile or rejecting, months or years prior to sexual aggression coming into the picture. If the child has another care-giver, he or she may be protective or alternatively not so, in either of the above two situations. In any event, perhaps because of a problem within the abuser himself, and/or because of his inability to form normal and satisfying adult relationships, combined often with a weakening of the usual taboos and restraints against sex between an adult and a child, the sexual abuse itself starts (Finkelhor, 1984).

The sexual misuse may start with excessive, physical contact, followed by fondling, and perhaps oral sexual contact much later on. Gradually, the contact will progress to intercourse, but this is uncommon in the early stages. From the victim's perspective, the activity may not seem abusive to begin with, and this, combined with the close relationship that may exist with the abuser, may be very confusing to the child. Younger children may think that perhaps all love and affection is similar to their experience and, furthermore, that this must happen to all children. In some part of themselves, they report feeling that it was somehow wrong, but at the same time not wishing to lose the emotional warmth they experienced when they were with the abuser, despite the high cost.

The child's cooperation at this stage is obtained by this gradual distortion of the care-giver/child intimacy. Perhaps the child will be told, ''don't tell your mother or she will get ill'', or ''this must be our special secret'', or ''if you tell, you will end up in a children's home, and never see your mother again'', or ''no one will believe you.'' Overt threats of physical harm are often not necessary, and the misuse of parental authority suffices to keep most victims silent. However, sometimes the threats are violent and threats of death or mutilation of either the child or someone whom the child loves, will be utilised to ensure secrecy (Lister, 1982). The feelings described by victims combine a mixture of fear, sexual stirring, and perhaps most of all the desire to be loved and attended to. Sometimes gifts and special favours accompany the threats, with the promise of a special position within the family for the child.

By this stage in the evolution of the sexual-abuse victim, the child's sexual feelings will have been harnessed and exploited by the abuser. The child now feels equally responsible along with the abuser, and it becomes even more difficult to tell anyone about his plight. Such children's self-image is a very negative one, and to confirm just how 'bad' they really are, they seem to take great pains to have their negative self-image reinforced at every opportunity. For example, they will reject praise, and search instead for punishment as negative reinforcement from adults. It is not surprising, then, that by adolescence, they have turned to numerous anti-social activities.

When a professional person, or perhaps a foster parent, first comes across a child who is at the end of this long-term adaptation, they often see a very unappealing child. Interviewing the child or young person in this unfortunate state of adaptation will, therefore, be very difficult, but perhaps an appreciation of the child's biography and an understanding of how they have survived, can help make these young victims more understandable.

The victims may show features of a post-traumatic stress disorder (see above). However, in the case of intrafamiliar sexual abuse, the stressor is a repeatedly occurring one. Hence, the victim may be reduced to a state of continual high anxiety which may be combined, paradoxically, with a state of inaction and a relatively frozen ability to create any change in her situation. Shengold (1967) has described this process very poignantly, and used the concept of a "rat person" to describe the effects of such prolonged overstimulation and abnormal stress. Peterson & Seligman (1983), from a somewhat different conceptual point of view, first of all studied the effects upon animals of subjecting them to overwhelming and relentless stress from which there was no escape. He termed the result of such prolonged and repeated stress 'learned helplessness'. Sometimes the professional onlooker may not be able to understand this process, and may disbelieve and respond with anger towards the human victim who has not protested more effectively. Such professional response is well recorded in the fields of spouse abuse (Pizzey, 1974) and in adult rape as well as in the child-abuse field (Tyler & Brassard, 1984).

After the disclosure has been made by the victims, the guilt connected with their participation in the abuse may intensify over the ensuing months. The feelings of guilt and personal responsibility may become combined with feelings of loss, and grieving for the emotional warmth that the abuser provided. At that stage, it is difficult for the victim to appreciate that the warmth and emotional availability were only provided at a price. The victims begin to feel that they caused the family's break-up, and perhaps the incarceration of the abuser. Retraction may be a frequent accompaniment at this stage (Summit, 1983).

The effect of the intervention system

In addition to the factors associated with the incest itself, there remain secondary effects of the system's response to the disclosure of the abuse (Giarretto, 1976). Included within these are the negative effects of multiple interviews that the child may have to suffer, insensitively performed medical examinations, prolonged foster-care placement with subsequent disruption of family bonds, and the break-up of the family. To these may be added the harmful pressure of repeated court appearances, frequently accompanied by delays and postponements. It has been recognised in many areas that the system's response does not have to be so cumbersome and inflexible, and co-ordinated treatment-oriented ways of responding to the disclosure of a child's sexual abuse have been designed. Giarretto (1976) pioneered such a program, and many others have followed. It appears that the emotional distress that may be caused by some of the above secondary influences is lessened by this type of system response. One of the purposes of this book is to contribute to the reduction of distress when children who have suffered trauma need to be examined psychologically.

2 The contribution of psychological research

The children's interviewer has to appreciate the developmental status of the child. This may be easy to dictate, but hard to achieve, for there are many theories available. An adherence to one particular school of thought without consideration of its critics or the contribution of other perspectives can blind one to the abilities of the individual child. Similarly, an absence of understanding about the differences in the capability of children of different ages can be a major handicap to the interviewer. There are good introductions to the topic of developmental psychology (see Donaldson, 1978; McGurk, 1975; Mussen et al, 1984) as well as critical, comparative reviews (e.g. Gelman, 1978). Most of the available theories of how children's minds develop describe how most children perform the majority of the time. They are useful general frameworks for appreciating an individual child, but there are certain limitations. For example, in the search for pattern and similarity, the differences between individuals can be lost. For this reason, any theory of the stages that children are said to negotiate while they grow up has to be paralleled by a knowledge of individual differences (see Kirby & Radford, 1976). There is not only a difference between persons, but also differences within the same child from one day to another to be taken into consideration when interviewing. Theoretical frameworks that include psychological and social development, can be useful, practical guides for what to expect of a child at a given age, provided they are used flexibly.

These general considerations should inform our interviewing approach and enable us to make use of some of the specific areas of research inquiry that are relevant to interviewing sexually abused children. These are discussed below, and include children's memory and suggestibility, their knowledge of the anatomy and function of sexual organs, and the study of children as witnesses to traumatic events. These specific areas will now be considered in more detail.

Children's memory

In this section, we refer to some of the findings of psychological research on a child's memory and its development through the child's life. A good introduction to the psychology of memory can be found in Brown *et al* (1983) Full reviews of the subject are available (e.g. Perlmutter, 1980). An excellent compilation of the major research findings in the area of children's memory and its application to children's ability to recall and relate that which they have experienced, is to be found in the book edited by Ceci *et al* (1987*b*). A shorter review that summarises the salient aspects for our field of concern is that by Davies *et al* (1986). From this area of research and inquiry, there emerge several themes which have practical importance for clinical interviews with children who may have been abused.

Over the last 10 years, we have realised that memory is not a unitary phenomenon akin to a video-tape residing somewhere in the depth of a human-being's brain, which, if only connected to the appropriate machine, can be successfully accessed. It is now generally accepted that no such tape recording exists, and that 'memory' consists of many elements that together comprise the overall idea of a memory. Instead of remembering a particular event as a single memory trace, we remember a series of fragments, which we piece together when we are required to recall and relate an event from the past. Furthermore, the memory itself is not a static phenomenon, but a process that is subject to change, dependent upon the circumstances under which a memory is initially created, and upon the psychological state of the individual during the period following the event itself.

Along with the somewhat rigid views of memory development that used to be in vogue, there was also the view that a child's memory progressed from a nil capability to an adult capability, which was regarded as the best available. Again, we now think that this was a simplistic model and, in fact, different facets of the process which we call memory develop at different rates. The poorer capability of children freely to recall events in detail is due to their lesser experience and understanding about the world in general and to the inept ways in which adults attempt to gain access to children's memories, as well as because of their insufficient grasp of language (Loftus & Davies, 1984). However, children may do better than adults in some memory tests. A study in 1947 (Allport & Postman) illustrates this very well. A group of adults and children were shown a film of a subway scene in which a black and a white man were engaged in a fight. In the scene, it was a white man who was menacing by holding a razor. Children, if they recalled this detail of the scene, did not confuse the colour of the man who was holding the razor – they correctly reported it was the white man. Adults viewing the same scene often erroneously reported that it was the black man wielding the razor. This study suggested that as human beings grow older they acquire an increasing number of prejudices that may actually affect how they perceive and remember the world that they live in. It also emphasises that the development of memory from infancy to adulthood should not be seen as a gradual achievement of the capability of adulthood. We should emphasise just which parts of memory develop, and which parts become more reliable, and which less reliable, with increasing age.

Another very interesting finding has been that young children who experienced events that made an impact upon them, even before they were able to speak, remembered those events accurately when they were 3 or 4 years old, and used their current language to relate the facts. This phenomenon even occurs without any rehearsal occurring between the time of the event and the moment when they recalled the event and related it to their parents (Todd & Perlmutter, 1980).

It is well known that the more time that has elapsed since an event was experienced, the less a person can recall about that event. This 'forgetting curve' occurs in both adults and children and in itself emphasises how important are the early statements that children or adults make soon after an event is experienced. In children, it has often been assumed that this process occurs to a greater extent than in adults. However, such research as we have suggests that the long-term capacity of children to remember past events is as good as adults.

What about the amount that a child recalls compared with an adult? In general, it is agreed that children recall less detail about any particular event than do their adult counterparts, and that this capacity gradually increases as children grow older. Thus, by the age of 10 or 12, children can become as adept as adults at remembering prior events. However, there are anomalies. For example, if elementary-school-age children and adults are compared on the quantity that they can recall on subject matter that they are very familiar with, then if anything, children do better than adults (Lindberg, 1980). It does appear, however, that children below the age of 5 recall less detail than do older children or adults (Goodman & Helgeson, 1985). As we have said, children, in general, recall less because their understanding of the world in general is not so well developed at earlier ages, and also because they may not have a sufficient grasp of language to be able to relate the events.

Children are often considered to have a problem putting events in the order in which they actually occurred. However, there is good evidence that, for events of central importance to children, their capacity to place events correctly in temporal order is surprisingly well developed, even for very young children (Gelman, 1979).

We know that the stress and personal impact of an event has an effect upon the memory process. We can distinguish between those events that have a personal poignancy for the child, and ones that may be considered a peripheral experience from the child's point of view. Central events are better recalled at a later date than are peripheral ones. (In this regard, peripheral events to the child may be very 'central' as far as the investigating adult is concerned and vice versa.) Clinical experience (Jones & Krugman,

1986; Pynoos & Eth, 1984) emphasises how important the personal impact of an event is on one's capacity to remember it. In addition, the added impact of the various pressures that bear upon the child, that were described in chapter 1, have to be taken into account. Sometimes children may take months before they are able to relate a traumatic event that they experienced, simply because of the fear and terror that causes them to suppress their memory (Lister, 1982; Russell, 1986; Summit, 1983).

Both adults and children may be suggestible, and their memories thereby distorted in the stage when they are retrieving their memory and recalling it for an interviewer. In both adults and children, the memory that is most susceptible to this alteration is that which is of less central importance or personal poignancy to the subject. Children, probably more than adults, are influenced potentially by the authority of the interviewer, and this implies that clinical interviewers should be careful not to overemphasise their authority in relation to children when they are interviewing them. Lastly, the suggestibility of an individual can be assessed in the clinical situation, as has been reported in individual case studies (Gudjonsson & Gunn, 1982; Jones & Krugman, 1986).

It is not uncommon to hear the view expressed that children are not able to distinguish between what really happened in objective reality and what happened in their dreams or thoughts. They are said to confuse fact and fantasy in this manner. The often-observed capacity for young children to relate the events of their dreams as though they were fact, is quoted as an example. However, children's dreams usually have the hallmark of fantasy about them, and can be easily related either to events in the child's experience or imagery that they have seen on a TV screen, etc. Johnson & Roley (1984) have reported on their experimental findings in investigating this very question. In general, these results and others indicate that young children may indeed have problems distinguishing their own thoughts and dreams from what actually did happen, but only in a specific way. That is, children do not appear to be more likely to confuse what they have dreamed of doing with what they actually saw; on the other hand, young children do have problems distinguishing between what they have actually done and what they have thought of doing. Thus, the idea that there is a generalised confusion in children between fact and fantasy does not have much support in the experimental literature, but in certain areas, children do show a relative inability to discriminate fact from fantasy. From the point of view of the courtroom, however, it is unlikely that a child will have a problem distinguishing what happened from their thoughts or dreams. On the other hand, they may report that they actually did something, when in fact they only dreamed or imagined that they had done so. It is of interest that children subjected to severe trauma will sometimes claim that they struck or defended themselves against the onslaught of their attacker, when in fact they wished and dreamed that they had done so, but had not been able to do so in reality (Pynoos & Eth, 1984; Terr, 1979).

Can children identify a face from memory? Photo-identification line-up is an accepted part of police investigations, but is not used very often in psychological investigations with children suffering from trauma. When exposed briefly to a person who is threatening, both adults and children do not identify their aggressor from a photo line-up with 100% accuracy. Reasons for this include the deleterious effect of stress upon their memory, the 'gun focus' effect, the effects of race upon face-recognition, and the influence of preconceived notions upon retrieval (Loftus & Davies, 1984). It seems, from the research that has been done, that children do as well as adults at this task after the age of approximately 6 years. However, most of the experiments that have been conducted have not tested the influence of the extended contact normally involved in a sexual assault on a child. In the experimental situation, 3-year-olds in one study (Goodman & Helgeson, 1985) had a less well-developed ability to identify a face accurately in a photo-identification line-up, than did 6-year-old children. In a study by Marin *et al* (1979), younger children were less inclined, however, to make false identification in a line-up experiment than were their adult counterparts. In an individual case study where a child was forcibly abducted and sexually abused, and then an attempt was made upon her life, the 3-year-old child made an accurate, unfaltering recognition of the face of her aggressor from a photo line-up (Jones & Krugman, 1986).

All the experimental studies have underlined the harm that can be done by leading techniques in the questioning of children. What are the possible distortions in children's memory? (Goodman & Helgeson, 1985; Loftus & Davies, 1984; Ceci *et al*, 1987*b*) First of all, various types of inquiry can be considered leading. A question may be plainly leading to the child, e.g. where did Daddy hurt you? Or, it may contain a bias toward one particular response as opposed to another, e.g. Daddy hurt you, didn't he? Further, the interviewer may use authority inappropriately, thereby intimidating the child and leading him to respond to the authority rather than the question itself. Additionally, the question may include a preconceived notion of the interviewer, e.g. because this child has been sexually abused, she must have been told not to tell, leading to the question, did Daddy tell you not to tell? Relentless probing for detail has been shown to be associated with error production (Dent, 1982). Research has shown that these types of questions do negatively affect the accuracy of the reply (Dale *et al*, 1978; King & Yuille, 1987). They affect the younger child even more than older ones. However, research has also shown that events of central importance to the child are much more robust and difficult to distort in the experimental situation. This leaves the practitioner with a dilemma, because events recalled after employing leading questions may have really occurred, or alternatively may have been distorted by the manner of questioning. Furthermore, after distortion, adults and children tend to persist with their now distorted memory, making future clarification exceptionally difficult (Loftus & Davies, 1984), although not impossible (Ceci *et al*, 1987*a*; Zaragoza, 1987).

We are, therefore, left with a problem of what to do when clinical circumstances imply the need to discover, but the child is silent. To go no further in questioning means to return the child to possible danger. While this is difficult for clinicians and the police, it may be better to accept that not all children will talk, than to use leading questions only to realise later on that the veracity of the information gathered is difficult to assess. Occasionally, leading questions are necessary, but only after open-ended questions have revealed no information. In this latter circumstance, it is the potential for harm to the child should abuse not be disclosed that should guide the decision as to whether to use leading questions. Less suggestible forms of leading questions are available and can be shown to reduce potential distortion compared with more strongly worded leading questions. Dale *et al* (1978) have provided an example of this, i.e. "did you see . . .?" is more leading than "did you see a . . . ?" which is, in turn, more leading than "were there any . . . ?"

There are implications of all these findings as how best to access children's memories. Some of these have been put to experimental test (Price, 1984). In this experiment, researchers employed the use of props and cues to young children's memory, and showed that the amount and accuracy of events recalled improves dramatically when appropriate props are available to the child. Examples of such props include small dolls' houses with figures, cars, aeroplanes, and toys, that may resemble those of their everyday experiences. Furthermore, the availability of props that may be similar to those involved in the incident of abuse can be helpful, and anatomically correct dolls are an example of such an aid. Lastly, there is good evidence that returning a child to the original context in which he was abused can significantly improve the accuracy and amount of information recalled. Naturally, this cannot always be done, because of potential emotional trauma to the child, but if it can be, then it may be a very useful aid to a child's memory. There is no evidence that using aids such as the above in any way distorts the child's memory, provided that leading questioning is avoided when presenting such props and cues.

Children's knowledge of sex

There have not been many studies of normal children's knowledge about sexual anatomy and physiology at different ages (see Melton *et al*, 1981; Rutter, 1980; and Waterman, 1986, for reviews). Children of elementary-school age, and younger, may have a poorly developed concept of their own sexual organs, and an even greater ignorance about those of the opposite sex. Studies have not so far discriminated those children who come from families with a more open approach to sexual education from those not so exposed. Additionally, the influence of factors such as the degree of personal nudity that is permitted in a household, and the presence of siblings of the opposite sex, have not been correlated with what an individual child at a certain age may know about sexual organs and how they work. Girls may have no language or concepts to enable them to discriminate between their urethral and vaginal areas during elementary-school years. They may only have a vague concept of penetration, even if it was a feature of their sexual abuse. It appears that pressure upon the vaginal introitus creates the feeling of penetration in girls under the age of approximately 7 years, even when vaginal penetration has not occurred. In a similar vein, up to the age of 10 years, children may have quite bizarre ideas about the origin of babies (Moore & Kendall, 1971). Some children have a fear of pregnancy following oral sexual contact with an adult, and their concern will need to be clarified by the interviewer. Ejaculation is beyond the comprehension of young children, who may describe it as "Daddy peed on me" or "yucky stuff came out". The paradox of the adolescent incest victim who, although tragically 'educated' to the point of full intercourse, is woefully ignorant about sexuality in general, is one that has struck many workers in this field (Porter *et al*, 1982)

There has been surprisingly little work done on 'normal touching' within families. Rosenfeld *et al* (1986) looked at patterns of behaviour in middle- and upper-middle-class families in California. They showed that some genital looking and touching occurred between adults and children in the majority of families. The touching was usually accidental, and in the context of bathing and dressing and normal family intimacy.

The child as a witness

There is conflicting opinion in the legal and psychological professions concerning how well children perform on the witness stand. There is also confusion as to whether children are harmed by testifying in open court, or whether it may prove a helpful vindicating process for the child to go through. It is probable that some children are helped psychologically by this public, authoritative vindication of their original statement (Berliner & Barbieri, 1984). On the other hand, there are other children who are psychologically harmed by the process of testifying. Both the issue of how well children do as witnesses, and that of the emotional trauma upon the child witness if he does testify, have been reviewed by Goodman (1984). We have studied sexually abused children who attended a criminal court to give evidence, comparing them with similar children who did not attend court. The preliminary results suggest that attendance at court is accompanied by greater psychological ill-effect over and above the impact of sexual abuse itself (Goodman & Jones, 1988).

3 Preliminary considerations

General principles

The overriding general principle is that of open-mindedness. We are not interviewing sexually abused children, but children who *may* have been sexually abused. Even when the level of suspicion is high, the interviewer has to maintain an open mind as to his or her professional conclusion until findings have been interpreted and the process of validation gone through (chapter 5).

Great care must be taken to remain open and honest throughout the interviewing process as in any constructive, supportive interaction with children. The style of this relationship may be quite different from the usual experience of the abused child with adults and can pave the way for future interviews. Although it is a natural tendency to attempt to protect children from pain and disappointment, it will harm them if they are told that "everything will be okay, don't worry". The child will quickly see through this, and see no reason to trust another in a long line of disappointing adults. In conjunction with such openness, it is important not to make promises that one cannot keep, and the child should not be prevented from knowing about the next steps. The child must know that a variety of circumstances may develop as a consequence of the interview, but that no guarantees can be made as to the outcome. Such consequences may be continued interviews, interviews with other adults, possible foster placements, etc.

Flexibility to change direction should be incorporated into the 'style' of the interviewer, so that allowance can be made for the child's special needs. There is no 'cookery book' of predictable questions and answers, nor a particular order in which they would be put. However, in every interview, there are specific content areas that have to be covered. These areas will vary from case to case. Prior to the session, the interviewer can delineate clear goals, which may be made into a checklist as an *aide memoire*. However, the child needs to unfold the details of the story at her own pace. This is a critical point, as often the interviewer is under a great deal of pressure to gather information needed to substantiate charges or secure the child's safety. The interview should proceed at the child's tempo, and not that dictated by the pressures of the 'system'. The more pressured the child feels, the less the interviewer will learn! The interviewer must be willing to accept the possibility that the first interview may not result in any information at all, or may involve a child who is not willing to share any information and refuses to speak. In many cases, further interviews are necessary. Some may continue after a short break of a few minutes or hours; others may reconvene after several days. The task of interviewing is made more difficult by each case and each child differing. An inability to substantiate clearly, or dismiss, an allegation of sexual abuse, should not be taken as an outright failure. The clinician has to accept the fact that not every interview goes as planned.

Personal aspects

Interviewing sexually abused children can evoke strong emotional reactions within the professional. Sexually abused children are often keenly attuned to these responses and feelings of adults, and may more quickly perceive the interviewer's disgust or sadness. Thus, the child may adapt her behaviour in the interview to lessen the reactions of adults, or may close up completely in order to avoid revealing emotion. As mental-health professionals, we like to think of ourselves as open, problem-free facilitators, but may nave to face the possibility that a child victim's account of sexual abuse may resonate some personal well-buried memories. If this is the case, there should be no shame attached to requesting that a colleague interview in one's place. Contemplation of such team support within an agency is critical if such openness is accepted. Feelings of horror, disgust, anger, and fear are commonplace. However, morbid curiosity is seldom discussed. The extreme of this interest may actually give the interviewer some type of vicarious reaction. How we deal with these and other feelings is a personal matter, but it would be folly to ignore them. We must be aware that such feelings can exist, and may affect a case's outcome if not taken into account. Thus, it is essential that an interviewer ponder these aspects of style, personal openness, and flexibility, as well as psychological factors, in pursuing a role as interviewer of sexually abused children. Further, caution must be given not to arrive eagerly at the issues of the investigation prematurely, or to succumb to the pressures of the system too readily. Such overenthusiasm tends to hamper the child's development of confidence in the interviewer and can lead to secondary distress. The interviewer must enter the session with an open mind and lack of bias; a 'don't yet know' stance (Goodwin *et al*, 1982) is critical if one is to gather important data that has such an impact on a child's future. Leading questions can lessen the usefulness of the interview when presented in court, and affect the entire process of evaluation but may also discourage the child's spontaneity and ability to trust the interviewer. Awareness of all these factors has to be incorporated into each interviewer's style.

Not every social worker, mental-health professional, medical practitioner, or police officer should expect to be proficient in the interviewing of children. Advanced knowledge of child development and psychological dynamics is required to interview these children accurately and skilfully. Professionals who are 'child-oriented' can reasonably develop these techniques, but many skilled clinicians are simply not adept at interviewing all sexually abused children. Some interviewers may be very understanding and knowledgeable with school-age children, but may be left helpless in the presence of a 3-year-old. These variations in skill are to be expected, and taken into consideration when assigning personnel to such projects. Variety within a cultural context must not be overlooked, as the interviewer has to understand the range in behaviour that is culturally accepted and practised.

There has been much deliberation as to whether the child victim should be interviewed by an adult of the same sex, by an adult of opposite sex from the alleged perpetrator, or by a male–female team. Unless the child's history is known prior to the interview, it may not be possible to arrange this for the child. In any case, the child's reaction to the interviewer may be helpful, and should be noted. Obviously, if the child is visibly frightened or extremely agitated in the presence of a particular sex, every effort should be made to replace the interviewer with someone with whom the child is more comfortable. Clinically it seems that the issue of the sex of the interviewer may be a more important factor with teenagers.

The setting

The choice of the setting for the interview may vary according to the urgency involved in a case and the availability of resources, as well as the nature of the allegations. In any case, the atmosphere in which the interview takes place is as critical as who conducts the interview. A playroom or space that is familiar to the child is preferable, but not always available. The interviewer can adapt many settings to enhance the child's comfort by creating a childlike atmosphere that incorporates the use of certain props, toys, and art materials. The combination of setting and materials helps to elicit verbalised accounts of abuse, as well as to provide an arena in which to observe the child's play. (For very young children, it is useful, if possible, to conduct the interview in the place where the abuse occurred.) The itinerant interviewer may carry a bag of such materials that can be used in a variety of settings. Suggested materials are listed in Appendix A.

Prior information

Access to prior records and history may prove helpful to the interviewer. It is best to know all the details available if an allegation has been made. This will often consist of a statement that a child has made to a friend or trusted adult. Basic information about the family is useful as well as some details of the child's everyday life, so that a starting point for the interview can be made. Additionally, what terms the child uses to describe body parts and sexual function, and if there are family names or terms of endearment that the child has for significant persons in his life should be discovered. Lastly, the family's style with respect to personal nudity, bathing, viewing sexually explicit material on video or in magazines, etc., should be explored. All this provides an important backdrop of information upon which to proceed with the interview. Having done this, the interviewer can note important information as an *aide memoire* to be taken into the session with the child.

Consent

When a standard mental-health assessment of a child is being conducted, parental consent is considered to be given implicitly. Such an assessment may well include screening questions concerning the possibility of abuse and trauma, including sexual maltreatment. Typical examples of such situations include the assessment of children whose symptoms raise suspicion of CSA, e.g. teenagers who have overdosed or self-mutilated. If a professional decides that a more facilitative approach is going to be needed during the interview (such as that outlined in chapter 4), then, ideally, parental consent should be sought. However, this may pose many practical difficulties if the parents themselves are directly or indirectly involved in the abuse of their child. Great care has to be exercised to avoid exposing the child to inordinate pressure from care-giving adults if full consent is sought in this way. If there is any doubt that consent will be forthcoming, or if it is refused, despite strong suspicion that CSA is a possibility, then the child's situation should be rapidly discussed with the local social-services department. There should not be a delay between the request for consent to the interview and the evaluation itself. If there is, inordinate parental pressure may be placed on the child to keep him or her silent. A child who is in care, or a ward of court, will require the consent of the local authority, or of the court, respectively. If the mental-health professional is in doubt, then the advice of the appropriate defence organisation will need to be sought as a matter of urgency. Difficulties such as those indicated above do occur, but often direct discussion with the parents about the need for a proper interview with the child will be accepted, and consent forthcoming. We generally try to obtain the assent of the child as well as formal consent from parent or guardian. We take a very similar approach with respect to consent about the method of recording the interview, e.g. audio- or video-taping.

Presence of parents

A common question asked is whether a parent or significant adult should be present. Consideration must be given as well to other persons who may be called on for further information, or who may need to be present for legal purposes. The child, obviously, is affected by numerous interviews, so that care must be given to eliminate the re-questioning and prolonged steps often present in such investigations. Generally, if the child is given easy access to the parent, and if the interviewer can see the child casually, with the parent, prior to the session, the child will feel comfortable enough to separate from the parent and talk with the interviewer alone. Practical suggestions would be that the child actually be shown where the parents will be waiting, and given permission to find them if necessary.

There may be unforeseen problems if a parent is present. The parent may appear to be supportive and non-abusive, but at the start of the interview this is unknown. We have seen so-called non-abusive parents become experts at non-verbally reminding the child to keep the secret while saying "tell the truth". Therefore, while the interviewer is in the stage of not fully understanding either child or family, it is best to see the child alone, if at all possible. If the parent must be present, then he must sit to one side, and be instructed not to help, nor to express his feelings or fears.

The only preparation that most children require is minimal, and along the lines that they are going to talk with 'X' about some things in the family. Specific preparation is best discouraged so as to avoid the child being coached, or his anxiety being elevated unnecessarily.

Recording the session

Documentation and recording of the interview can be done with a variety of methods; available resources and agency requirements affect the choice. Though often distracting to the child as well as to the interviewer, some note-taking is required to describe the process. Audio recording obviates the necessity for extensive note-taking, but has to be complemented by written comments describing the child's non-verbal behaviour. Video recording provides the most complete form of record. Video recordings can be very helpful for the clinician, enabling him or her to review the interview at a later date. Video is not a panacea however (MacFarlane, 1985). Without first-class equipment, sound and picture clarity may leave much to be desired. Additionally, there are implications for confidentiality, and for storage of tapes. It is generally considered that the tapes are potentially subject to laws of discovery, and therefore have to be stored and not erased, in case there is future legal action. Clinicians have to consider if the use of video-tape is likely to reduce spontaneity or even frighten the child. Those making video records primarily for the purpose of availability for court purposes should liaise with the local Crown Prosecution Service in order to discuss format, storage, and the labelling requirements, as well as aspects of interview style. Consent and assent should be sought before video recording. In the USA, video-taped recordings have proved to be a frequent catalyst to positive legal decisions on behalf of children, by offering evidence that is difficult to articulate secondhand. The use of video-tapes has lessened the necessity for children to be subject to repeated interviews, and appears also to have lessened the need for the child to give evidence in court.

Which professional should interview the child?

Different professionals approach CSA with separate professional responsibilities. Thus, the police are concerned primarily with crime detection, although they are likely to be concerned also with child safety and protection. The social-services department is mainly concerned with child protection and safety, and whether such safety has to be secured through court orders. Psychiatrists and psychologists are concerned with the influence of sexual abuse upon the person's development. General medical practitioners, paediatricians, and health visitors are similarly concerned, but may also be involved with assessing the child's physical growth and development, as well as any physical abnormalities associated with sexual abuse. All these professionals come across children who might have been, or are currently being, sexually abused. However, a single approach to interviewing such children is not appropriate for all these professional groups. Most paediatricians, general practitioners, and health visitors need a screening-interview approach that is suitable for everyday practice. Like many other medical practitioners, they meet children for whom sexual abuse is one possible factor within a differential diagnosis list. In overt cases, referral to the local social-services department will be necessary, when the approach set out in chapter 4 would be appropriately followed. In other cases, where mild suspicion of the possibility of CSA exists, a series of screening questions may be a useful approach for different circumstances (see below). Our questions are not as probing as some of those suggested by Leventhal et al (1987), but there are many similarities. Additionally we do not recommend a leading-question style when only mild suspicion exists (Kolvin et al, 1988). The questions that follow are presented as possible approaches. We abhor the cookery-book approach, which is inflexible to individual situations. The questions should be taken as possible approaches, to be adapted by the individual practitioner and applied to situations where a screening approach is necessary, but a convenient phrase does not come to mind. In such situations, a few set phrases can be useful.

General questions

General questions interposed with standard talk with the child directed towards discipline in the home, sleeping arrangements, bathing arrangements and privacy, may be useful questions that will in themselves suggest whether further assessment is necessary. The child's silence and reluctance to discuss such matters may be just as instructive as positive remarks made. Further general questions may involve examples such as "Is there anything that you feel unhappy about, that you'd like to talk to me about?". Other approaches can involve questions about touching, such as the following: "Has anyone touched you on private parts of your body – and made you feel uncomfortable?". It may be possible to pick up on hints, early warnings (see chapter 1) or other information known to the practitioner in advance. General questions can then be linked in with such knowledge.

Questions while examining the child's genitalia

This is often a very fruitful time to pose questions directly asking the child whether anyone has "played games/touched you down here – has that ever happened to you?" or "can you tell me how you got sore down here?". A child who has been abused will often experience considerable relief at the opportunity to talk about such matters.

Questions that can be addressed to the parent (care-giver) while the child is within earshot

This can be a useful facilitating approach where the above approaches have not led to any positive responses, although the child's non-verbal responses may leave the practitioner in considerable doubt as to whether sexual abuse may indeed have occurred. In such situations, the possibility of sexual abuse as one of the differential diagnostic possibilities can be plainly and straightforwardly put to the care-provider along with the other possibilities that the clinician is considering. However, we have to be cautious when using this technique, because the care-provider may subsequently apply pressure on the child to remain silent. This can occur through the care-giver being the abuser, or being in collusion with the abuser.

Having talked to the child in this way, the clinician must inform the general practitioner that such questions have been asked of the child. It may well be necessary to see the child, as well as his or her parents, again. Additionally, screening approaches such as those discussed above cannot be left to another professional. Screening is usually needed at the time it is contemplated, not later. In many cases, the result of having utilised a screening approach would be referral to other specialist agencies. However, valuable initial information will have been obtained from the above approach and must be carefully recorded (in whatever way is appropriate and available) so that it can form part of the child's record.

Considering who should undertake the more detailed interview (described in chapter 4), the assessment of a case of possible sexual abuse will be the first step of the intervention process. The assessment will cover not only whether abuse happened, but also what effect it has had upon the child's functioning. Thus, a broad picture of the child's status will be obtained. Different professionals will naturally bring a different emphasis to this, however. For example, child psychiatrists and psychologists will be particularly interested in whether, and in what way, abuse has affected the child's and family's development. On the other hand, a police officer or social worker from an intake team will be primarily concerned with whether abuse has happened. However, a clean divide between whether abuse has happened, and if it has, what effect it has had, is often impossible to achieve even if it is thought to be desirable. Thus, the child psychiatrist may well have to discover whether abuse has happened in order to know if it is of aetiological significance with respect to the child. Similarly, an intake social worker must concern him- or herself with what effect abuse has had, when making child-protection decisions, even though the emphasis may be upon whether abuse has happened. Generally speaking, child mental-health professionals do not interview well children, who are not disturbed, in order to see if they have been abused. Exceptions to this include children under the age of 5, mentally handicapped children, and those who are caught in divorce and custody cross-fire (Jones & Seig, 1988). Social workers and police officers do interview psychologically well children, in order to see if a child requires protection, or if a crime has been committed.

Whatever the main focus of the initial assessment, the focus must be broad enough to allow an insight to be gained into the emotional climate that the child lives in, coupled with some information as to how the child perceives himself in relation to his or her family. Similarly, the child is assessed individually and within the context of the family. Family members will be seen for assessment too. As the assessment process progresses, the relationship that develops between the interviewer and child can serve as a catalyst to future treatment. In fact, this initial foundation is a crucial stage, and may well determine the success or failure of any subsequent intervention.

The emphasis in this publication is on assessing whether abuse has happened. The assessment of the effect of such abuse upon the psychological development of the victim, or upon other family members, or whole-family functioning has not been considered. An assessment-interview approach such as that outlined in chapter 4 should not have to be repeated numerous times. Local planning combined with careful documentation and recording should preclude the need for unnecessary repetition.

4 The interview itself

An individual who engages in the challenge of interviewing sexually abused children develops his or her own techniques over time, and chooses to develop a certain 'style' and structure within the interview itself. The support of a team or colleagues within an agency or department are essential as one develops. Supervision and/or consultation is a must not only as the clinician starts in the area of sexual abuse, but throughout his or her career. Many who have tried to continue in this field without these emotional and professional supports, have become less effective over time.

Structure of the interview

There is a range of opinion within the field concerning whether or not the interview should be structured, and if it should, to what extent. At the one extreme, there are proponents of a rigidily pre-planned format (e.g. White *et al*, 1986). In these and similar protocols, the child is steered back 'on track' if he or she strays from the planned format. Our interview has a specific aim and purpose (that of discovering if CSA has occurred or not) and has a series of stages to it, but its precise flow and format is adapted to the individual child. Additionally, the choice of materials used to help facilitate the session is based upon clinical judgement and those materials chosen are tailored to the individual. For example, a 'talking' interview may be used with one child, the use of dolls and toys with another, similarly aged, child.

Our series of stages are as follows:

1. starting the interview;
2. inquiry about sexual abuse;
3. facilitation;
4. free play;
5. gathering specific detail;
6. the closing space.

Not all child interviews need all the stages. In addition, the order may well vary from child to child. However, for ease of instruction and description, the above format is used to describe the process. Some specific issues, e.g. leading questions, and the use and misuse of anatomically correct dolls are described, where appropriate. Lastly, with regard to structure, it is recognised that certain sections of a typical interview do require pre-planning. Thus the interviewer is recommended to memorise a mental 'checklist' of items to be covered during the detailed phase of the interview. Additionally, it is helpful to have rehearsed a pre-planned approach to the use of degrees of facilitation prior to interviewing. Also, those professionals who are just starting to interview children may find it useful to have some rehearsed introductory enquiry phrases in mind and/or a pre-planned approach to the closing phase, so that they do not become lost for words or forget the important necessity to close a session in a humane way for a child. Again, we stress that this approach is quite separate from the cookery-book approach (King & Yuille, 1987). and the structure is presented as a guide and by way of an example.

1. Starting the interview

There are various ways to establish rapport and engage the child's interest. The interviewer can explain who he is, and describe his role. Children may respond to the questioning of their perception as to why they are being interviewed. This will often break the ice, and allow any misconceptions to be clarified. It also establishes the interviewer as a straightforward person who does not indulge in secrets or devious methods. At some stage, but not necessarily the starting one, the issue of confidentiality of information is likely to emerge. This gives the interviewer the opportunity to tell the child who will hear the results of the interview and with whom the interviewer must share information. The interviewer avoids promising confidentiality if it cannot be assured. Paradoxically, most children will respond to this approach even if they initially sought total secrecy.

Acknowledgement of the difficulty of such a session may be given in an empathic or non-intrusive manner at any stage during the interview, in order to build rapport with the child. During the interview, we may need to pause and reflect upon such a difficulty, letting the child know that she will not be pushed, prodded, or coerced into surrendering information. We want the child to know and feel that she has given her assent to the process, as well as the consent that may well have been obtained from parents or guardians. The interviewer's anxiety to discover if the child has been abused can result in too eager an approach, confounding the result and raising the child's anxiety.

There is no place in this investigative interview for teaching children about the 'correct' words for sexual organs, or places that are 'private', nor for lectures about what it is that adults should and should not do. Our aim is simply to find out if anything of a sexually inappropriate nature happened, and if so, exactly what that was.

Generally, we do not discuss specific matters too early in the interview. General conversation, including issues not related to the abuse, may be used initially to build some confidence with the child. Questions at this stage about school, friends, and hobbies are typically non-threatening and encourage spontaneity. It is important, however, not to draw out the preliminaries for too long a period of time, particularly with adolescents, as they will become bored. One girl remarked, after several minutes of what she perceived as small talk, ''when are we going to talk about IT?''

2. *Inquiring about sexual abuse*

The question of sexual abuse itself can be raised generally at first, with subsequent questions becoming increasingly specific. This principle can be applied to children of most ages. The technique of starting with general questioning can be compared with the start used in suicide questioning. For example, in the latter instance, one might inquire ''How low have you been?'' followed later by ''Have you ever wished you were not alive?'' Eventually, the questions lead to asking which methods of suicide have been considered, etc. We can approach the question of sexual abuse with children in a similar vein.

It can be difficult to move from generally gaining rapport to inquiry about sexual abuse. Care needs to be taken so as not to change demeanour suddenly and raise the child's anxiety.

Quite how we inquire about CSA depends upon the type of suspicion that has led to the current assessment. Broadly there are four categories: (a) something the child has said; (b) an adult's suspicion about a place or person; (c) physical disease; (d) or the child's behaviour. Initial inquiry questions are guided by the type of suspicion. Typical approaches might be as follows:

(a) Something the child has said.

''I have spoken with X, and it sounds as though a lot of things have been happening in your family. Can you tell me a little bit about that?''

''You told me that you were talking with me today because someone in your family did something that he shouldn't have* – can you tell me a little bit more about that?''
[*Substitute here whatever it was the child said when answering why the interview was taking place (see *Starting the interview*, above).]

''Your mummy said you had some worries about being touched on private parts of your body – can you tell me about that?''

(b) Adult suspicion about a place or person.

"Tell me who looks after you when your mum goes out . . . . What things do you like to do with (babysitter) . . . . Anything that you don't like doing with (babysitter)?"

"X told me that you don't like it when Uncle John comes to stay at your house – can you tell me about that?"

(c) Physical disease (see page 22).

(d) Behaviour. Behaviour change or type (e.g. sexualised behaviour) may raise suspicion of CSA. There may be no other clues, such as those above, to allow a lead into initial inquiry. Raising concerns about CSA may then be quite difficult for the interviewer to do without being fairly direct. These are some possible approaches.

(i) Inquiry about the child's symptoms (anxiety, depression, nightmares), for example:

"Tell me about the things you've been worrying about."

"What happens in your scarey dreams?"

"When you were playing like that with Fred, . . . have there ever been any other times when you've played games like that?"

"Has anyone ever played games like that with you?"

(ii) General inquiry about family, or friends. Here it is possible to use a family drawing to discover who the child likes and/or dislikes, and for what reasons.

If these opening questions do not result in a spontaneous account, one might inquire more specifically along the following lines, either directly or after having identified body parts on a doll or drawing:

"Has any one touched you on your body in ways that made you feel uncomfortable?"

"Has anyone touched the private parts of your body – like where your swimsuit goes – and made you feel uncomfortable?"

3. Facilitation

If the child indicates that he or she may have been sexually abused, or if the interviewer has a strong basis for suspecting that CSA may have occurred, then more enabling techniques are called for. In this phase, as in others, the approach used with the individual child must be a clinical judgement. We will describe various approaches that we have found useful, and which have a rational basis for their use in the studies that have been conducted (see chapter 2).

Methods of facilitation include the use of facilitating questions and the use of toys and materials. It seems to us, clinically, that an all-important element of facilitation is the creation of an atmosphere of acceptance and safety throughout the interview. Additionally, the adoption of a relaxed yet purposive style, appears to us to be important. It is interesting that studies of error production in experimental situations with children have begun to highlight the relevance of these issues of style and general manner (Dent, 1982; King & Yuille, 1987; Tully & Cahill, 1984). It may well turn out, after further study, that these and similar issues will be more relevant to the likelihood that the child will make errors of recall than the type of question *per se*. A further aspect of interviewing style, which is probably crucial, is the avoidance of embarrassment, disgust, shock, or aversion. Similarly, the interviewer should avoid vicarious interest in the subject matter (we have had children say to us "All he wanted was to hear what my Dad did and get turned on by it; so I shut up . . . wasn't going to tell him anything").

With these caveats, the specific methods of facilitation are now discussed, dealing first of all with questioning approaches. If open-ended questions produce no answers, and the interviewer remains suspicious, then more enabling questions may be used. Questions can be phrased in a permission-giving or enabling way. Objective or direct questions may be posed to the child. Questions such as these provide a mild-to-moderate degree of facilitation, depending on the context or style in which they are used. Some examples are as follows:

> "Did anyone, even a grown-up who you are close to, ever touch the private parts of your body, like where your swimsuit goes?"
>
> (Direct question)

> "I talk to a lot of children and sometimes to children who have been touched on private parts of their bodies. It can help to talk about things like that. Has anything like that ever happened to you?"
>
> (Permission-giving and ending with a direct question)

> "Some kids are touched in private places on their body by people who are close to them, like someone in their family who they know very well. Has anything like that ever happened to you?"
>
> (Permission-giving and ending with a direct question)

Questions such as these avoid suggesting to the child a particular person as a possible abuser. On the other hand, if one were to ask, "Did Daddy touch you . . . ?", the result could be highly misleading.

At the other end of the scale of facilitation lie questions which involve a marked degree of facilitation. Such approaches include the either/or format (multiple choice) or the hypothetical question. Examples are:

> "Were you touched on the (child's word for vulval area) or your knee?"
> "Did Daddy touch you on your pee-pee or another part of your body?"
>
> (Either/or format)

"If Daddy had touched you on your pee-pee, how would that have felt?"
(Hypothetical)

Sometimes the either/or format is useful, but usually only after the child has indicated something and subsequently become stuck for words. The hypothetical format is not one we use, except very rarely, because of the problems of subsequent interpretation. We feel that even if the answer is affirmative, one is still left wondering if maltreatment has taken place or not. The format may be helpful in enabling the child who has already disclosed something during the interview, but has then become too fearful to proceed to talk (Leventhal *et al*, 1987).

Other questioning styles can be facilitating, especially those that reduce the child's anxiety. For example, circular questioning is a useful approach. In this method, the interviewer talks around and around the focus of the question, dwelling on items that do not elevate anxiety, with a style that is anxiety-reducing. Then, at an opportune moment, an aspect of CSA is inquired about.

If the child says yes to facilitative styles of questioning such as those in the examples above, the question which follows it needs to be put in an open-ended style. For example, if the child replies "yes" to any of the above questions, then the next question should be along the lines of "Could you tell me a bit more about that?".

Language

There are certain 'dos' and 'don'ts' with respect to language used in the interview. We use the child's own terms for sexuality and sexual organs (see pages 14–19). 'Why' questions are generally avoided, as they are confusing for the child. The interviewer's 'why' questions are likely to be interpreted by a sexually abused child as imputing guilt, e.g. "Why didn't you ask for help sooner?" "Why did he do that to you?", etc. Sentences should be kept short, specific questions contain one idea, and double questions avoided. Questions containing a double negative are especially confusing to children. Pronouns are better avoided, and names used in their place, e.g. "Did Daddy do anything else?" is preferable to "Did he do anything else?"

Dealing with fear

Children who have been sexually abused are usually required by the abuser to keep silent about their experience. The corollary that all secretive, silent children are sexually abused, is not the case. Hence, we approach the reticent, fearful child who may appear to be hiding something, with an open mind. Such a child may be hiding an abuse secret, or may be concealing another unknown concern. Not all silent children are 'in denial' or 'not yet disclosing', but some are. How can we help the latter children to reveal abuse while avoiding our professional suggestion and influence? Some general principles in this section are described, and specific methods that may be helpful outlined in the following section.

If children show signs of fear, sadness, or guilt, one must acknowledge that and attempt to empathise with them. The child should be asked if he feels uncomfortable, and then discussion with him about how clarifying what has happened will help him in the end, even if it causes difficulty in the short term, should take place. (It should not be promised, however, that all will be well if they are able to talk about their abuse, because in reality, matters may become worse in the short term.) Acknowledging that it is hard to talk can be facilitating with a reticent child. Asking the child what he is scared about can relieve anxiety in a similar fashion.

It is often more productive, when the child is showing signs of resistance, to return at intervals to the traumatic subject throughout the course of the interview, rather than pursuing the sexual-abuse theme relentlessly.

Free play is an important element of the interview, especially with younger children, and can be very helpful with fearful youngsters. Periods of free play may occur at any time during the session. We prefer to avoid pre-planning a set period of free play, and tend instead to have episodes of free play with the dolls' house, drawing materials, or larger dolls, throughout the interview. Some practitioners recommend a period of play without the interviewer present, at the end of their session (e.g. Jampole & Weber, 1987).

Direct gaze fixation is often too intrusive for children, and various techniques are described below that include within their benefits the factor of avoiding eye-to-eye gaze. In the following section, we describe different techniques that we have found helpful in eliciting detail. These have the advantage of using materials familiar to the child, and they are methods through which children can show or illustrate to us their concerns. These techniques reduce the sense of intrusion and help the child to relax. The most intrusive style imaginable is that of two chairs facing each other, with the interviewer and child in close proximity. If one adds to this scene an authoritarian manner and an insistence upon verbal communication solely, many children will remain silent, or even worse, produce unreliable answers (Goodman, 1984).

Similarly, **touch** may carry ambiguous implications for a sexually abused child. Even a well-intentioned, comforting gesture can be interpreted by the child as threatening, or alternatively, provocative. Therefore, an interviewer should exercise great caution before incorporating physical contact into the interview.

Use of toys and play materials

The following techniques are suggested as useful ways to encourage a child to discuss any abuse that may have occurred. These techniques may also be useful methods to supplement and elicit further detail once a child has said that he or she was sexually abused.

Small figures, with accompanying dolls' houses, and small cars, are useful props with which children suffering from trauma can indicate their experience (see Appendix A). Once a child begins to play with these figures, he or she may be gently encouraged to talk about their play. Joining with the child while avoiding overintrusion is a key issue at this stage. If premature identification of the figures and actors is required by the interviewer, the child may well leave that particular play scene and embark upon another one. Children may also relabel the characters during the course of a play sequence and say what they are doing out loud, and if this occurs, they should be permitted to do so. Here again, we attempt to help children expand upon their play, but we avoid directing it, if at all possible.

Puppets (both glove and face) may be used to re-enact situations that the child has difficulty recalling with words alone. If, for example, the child is getting stuck, then one can say that ''it is difficult to talk isn't it'', and that sometimes it is easier for him if he can talk through a puppet figure. Once he gets the idea that he can talk through a puppet figure, then instead of the puppet talking to the interviewer, it may be easier for the child to have his puppet talk to the one which the interviewer holds. In this way, the conversation can become less threatening to the child. With puppets and with similar techniques, where the child uses play to represent real life, we need to bring the child from the allegorical towards talking in the first person about his or her actual experiences.

Larger dolls, between 12 and 18 in long, can be useful props to enable children to describe where and how they were abused. They can also be useful to help indicate how the perpetrator approached and touched them. Both ordinary, commercially available dolls and anatomically correct dolls can be used for this purpose.

Art is widely employed by many evaluators (Goodwin, 1982; Naitore, 1982; Stember, 1980). The child may be asked to draw himself, or perhaps

Fig. 1. A 7-year-old girl's sexualised drawing of her father; detail of ''his penis'' at the right

Fig. 2. A child's self-portrait

Fig. 3. A sexually abused girl's drawing of her family

his family doing something together (kinetic family drawing), or may be asked to draw siblings. Some evaluators encourage children to draw the alleged perpetrator also. When we are using art in this way, flexibility becomes very important, and a variety of media can be used. For example, some children enjoy using clay or Play do®, and can sculpt their experience for the interviewer. These techniques can be very useful with children who do not want to talk about the experience, or are feeling very reticent. Having the interviewer and the child involved in drawing or using clay alongside each other, can be a useful technique and put the child at sufficient ease to disclose their misuse. Winnicott (1971) used a somewhat similar process when interviewing children he saw for consultation on paediatric hospital wards, naming it the "squiggle" technique. With this method, he passed a rudimentary drawing first to the child and then the child would do one for him – each would then complete the drawing in the way that they wanted to, thereby allowing an element of free association to occur between the two of them.

When art is used in this way, children may express overtly sexualised themes in their drawing. (Fig. 1). They then can be asked to talk about their drawing. Art may also illustrate how poorly the child feels about himself (Fig. 2). Family drawings may reveal important themes concerning the child's position within the family, her view of the role of other family members, and sometimes her sense of disappointment as to the emotional unavailability of parents. Figure 3 shows a family of three – a sexually abused girl and her father occupy the house while her mother is "sleeping under the pond". Drawing can be a useful technique to allow small children to indicate what part of their body was hurt or harmed. Figure 4 illustrates the use of this method with a 2-year-old child who was asked to show on

Fig. 4. A 2-year-old girl's indication of abuse

the drawing where she had been molested. She had previously said that her
stepfather had hurt her and had pointed with her finger to her genitals. The
child then became very reticent and the interviewer suggested that perhaps
it would help to draw a picture of herself and her stepfather in order to help her.
The interviewer then drew the little girl while she drew her stepfather. Then,
the girl made dots, followed by a firm line drawn upwards from her crotch
to indicate where she had been touched.

Line drawings are useful to enable children to describe abuse. Simple
line drawings done by the interviewer or commercially available ones can
be used for this purpose. Groth's Anatomical Drawings (see Appendix B)
are designed to be photocopied, allowing an individual child's indication
of abuse to be recorded and filed. The *Red Flag/Green Flag People* booklet (see
Appendix B) has been used by many interviewers, as it develops the idea
of appropriate and inappropriate touching before finally asking the child
where he was touched and in what way.

Sometimes, with an older child, picturing a traumatic event as though
projected into the distance through a window, with both interviewer and
child turned and looking out together, can be a useful technique. Milton
Erickson used many methods similar to this to communicate with his patients
(Haley, 1973).

Anatomically correct dolls

Various terms have been used to describe anatomically correct (AC) dolls
(e.g. anatomically detailed, anatomically complete, sexually explicit). These
dolls are rag dolls with genitalia, body hair, and bodily orifices all present.

They are available in different racial styles, and some have tongues, fingers, and detachable body hair. In the past, there have been criticisms that the genitalia have been disproportionately large, but this has been less of a problem with recent dolls (Appendix B). They are 'big business'; as may be evidenced by the slick marketing on the stalls of some CSA conferences. All self-respecting agencies who interview children consider they must have at least one set. But are they necessary? We consider that they can be useful in certain circumstances, but should not be the mainstay of all evaluative assessments of all young, potentially abused children. Clearly, with anatomically correct dolls, one can be more precise when children are indicating and showing where they were misused, but such dolls may also be intrusive and somewhat frightening for some children. Until recently, because there were only pilot studies on the actions of normal or non-abused children when playing with anatomically correct dolls (Jampole & Weber, 1987; White *et al*, 1986), there had to be caution in interpreting children's play with them. When a child appears to be indicating sexualised contact with anatomically correct dolls, they should be asked who the people are, and what is happening, etc. What the children do with the dolls can help augment their statements, but not too much weight should be placed on the play exclusively. Despite assertions to the contrary, there has been no convincing evidence to support the notion that AC dolls *per se* cause spurious accounts. Aman & Goodman (unpublished data) tested the notion that the combination of AC dolls and suggestive questions was potentially error-prone. Their careful design consisted of a group of children interviewed with AC dolls, another with ordinary dolls, and a third without any dolls. The 3-year-olds were more suggestible, overall, than the 5-year-olds, but the group with AC dolls did no worse than those interviewed without them. The 'AC-doll group' did not produce false or spurious reports. For the 5-year-olds, dolls of either sort produced better results than free recall.

At present, the best uses of anatomically correct dolls are with pre-, and barely-verbal children when asking them to demonstrate abuse, and to provide a further medium through which a child of any age can describe abuse if she has already done so by words or using a drawing. Additionally, if she has described abuse to the extent she is able, and shows a need to demonstrate further detail, the use of dolls may be indicated (e.g. Jones & Krugman, 1986). Even in these conditions, 'ordinary' dolls can be equally useful in most situations. It is not recommended that anatomically correct dolls be used as the initial, sole means of inquiry.

It is suggested that a set of dolls be available, yet out of sight of the child, and that 'ordinary' rag dolls and dolls suitable for the school-aged child (see Appendix A) be used in preference to AC dolls. If AC dolls **are** brought out for the child, something such as: "These are dolls that look like people really look like underneath. . . ." should be said. Whether the child spontaneously explores the doll should be noted. They should be used to encourage recall and speech, in preference to relying on the child demonstrating events remembered. The child should be permitted to change the identity of the doll as the interview progresses, and encouraged to talk about the doll without pressure, leaving plenty of time for free play. The child then becomes confident and at ease with the dolls. At this stage, a process of naming the doll's bodily parts may be gone through, after which the child is asked if anyone has touched him or her, here (pointing to the doll's genital area). After this stage, more detail is requested, attempting always to encourage spontaneity in the child. The doll should not be named, e.g. "Let this be Daddy, etc.". By contrast, the child should be allowed to talk and demonstrate at his or her own pace. If the child has not already indicated who the doll represents, he may be asked "Is this doll like someone you know?" (NB, not, "Is this Daddy?"). If the child says "Daddy", more detail is requested (see *Gathering specific detail* below). The child is permitted to change the identity of the doll as the interview progresses, and the dolls are used to encourage recall and speech in preference to the demonstration of events remembered by the child.

Leading questions

The issue of leading questions is a controversial one in this field, as assessment interviews may lead to the filing of criminal charges and civil court actions to protect the child. Some professionals erroneously assert that any question other than the most open-ended is 'leading'. This is incorrect, and several points will be raised here. First, there is a clear relationship between the degree to which the question is subjective (thereby potentially leading the child to an answer already suggested by the interviewer), and the subsequent distortion of memory and recall. Both research (see pages 13–14) and clinical experience attest to this. Thus, those suggestions made by the interviewer that employ maximum use of authority, and that ask questions such as "Did Daddy touch you here?", are particularly troublesome compared with those recommended in the section above. Second, the context or timing of the subjective question (potentially leading) has to be examined. The questions that precede and follow the subjective question are of great importance. In the recommended sequence, initial questions are open-ended, with subsequent ones becoming more specific during the course of the interview, until, finally, the subjective question is used, e.g. "some kids are touched. . ." If the child says "yes", the next question should be open-ended. If the child's answer merely recapitulates the suggestion inherent in the subjective question, only limited conclusions may be drawn. If the child describes detailed sexual acts with specificity and emotion, we can be much more confident that he or she has been abused. Third, there is a major difference between an interview which contains one or two leading questions, and one which contains nothing but leading questions. The latter has been aptly described as a 'driven' interview.

4. Free play

Some authors recommend that a specific period of free play is incorporated into the interview with the young child (e.g. Vizard *et al*, 1987; Jampole & Weber, 1987). We have found this period to be useful in certain cases, if it is possible to incorporate it. Most of the authorities who recommend this phase are particularly concerned to observe the child's free play with anatomically correct dolls. Some sexually abused children re-enact or demonstrate sexual activities during free play, whereas the non-abused do so less frequently (Jampole & Weber, 1987; Glaser, unpublished data). However, as already noted in the section on anatomically correct dolls, this observation does not constitute a 'test' as to whether abuse has occurred. If re-enactment is seen, then it may corroborate something the child has already said, but does not stand alone.

We do not routinely use anatomically correct dolls in our interviews, and if we do, there are often periods of the session when there is no talking with the young child, just play with the interviewer present in the room. If the child does not appear to demonstrate something specifically sexual, he or she is then encouraged to talk about it at the time. Thus, our use of free play is usually as periods which are interspersed with the general flow of the interview. Occasionally, a specific period of free play is used, with the interviewer leaving the room and observing from behind a one-way screen. This is usually done if facilitation has not enabled a child to talk specifically, but the interviewer has a strong basis to suspect that CSA has indeed occurred (Kolvin *et al*, 1988). In such circumstances, the change of format to free play can prove useful.

Behavioural observations

Direct observations of the child's behaviour and his use of play are critical and as important as the spoken material. (For good reviews of the range and meaning of children's play, see Garvey, 1977; Rosenblatt, 1980; Rubin *et al*, 1983; Tizard & Harvey, 1977). Assessment of the effects of the abuse and of the experience itself cannot be done wholly by examination of content only, but should include the interpretation of the behaviour in the interview. The interviewer documents behavioural changes, mood shifts, etc., as they relate to subject matter. The following types of behaviour should be noted:

What is the change in mood? What topic caused the mood to change?

What topics precipitate a change in behaviour?

What topics distract the child?

What topics cause the child to make attempts to distract the interviewer?

What topics does the child avoid altogether?

What does the child's affect tell you? What does his body language tell you?

What play materials does the child choose? What does he avoid?

In general, how does the child cope with the anxiety of the interview?

How does the child interact with the interviewer? Is he appropriately distant, too friendly, etc.?

Does the child change grammatic tenses or pronouns, or use word substitutions?

These observations can be documented by taking notes or by reviewing a video-tape of the session. If audio-taping the session, these shifts in behaviour and affect need to be recorded, or the interviewer will lose those critical details. This is particularly relevant with young children who may be pre-verbal, or choose to remain silent.

5. Gathering specific detail

Once the child begins to talk about being sexually abused in answer to questions such as these, one needs to enable them to give a fuller account. Following the child's lead by allowing them to give their story at their own pace, with their own words, is the key issue at this point. Caution should be exercised here to avoid the use of suggestion or any leading form of question, as the interviewer can become overanxious, and in his or her eagerness, dampen the child's spontaneity. One has to be cautious to modulate one's own emotional response both in this way and with respect to the content and details which the child may relate. For example, one 5-year-old girl recanted her story quickly when she gauged the emotional response of her interviewer, and some weeks later said "I said it didn't happen, because she looked so sad". Sometimes the interviewer may be disgusted or horrified at the violence or perversity of the abuse that the child relates. We have to remain aware that abused children are highly tuned to the emotions of others.

There are certain specific areas to be explored in addition to the details of the sexual abuse alone. To understand better the effects of the abuse on the child, to plan the appropriate intervention for the child and his family, and to provide the court with as much substantiating information as possible, the interviewer should attempt to gather as much data as possible regarding the following areas:

What was the intent and emotion of the perpetrator?

Was there violence involved? Were any threats used? What were they? What were the words that the perpetrator used?

Where and when did the abuse take place?

(This is difficult for pre-school-age children, but connecting the abusive event to Christmas, birthdays, holidays, trips, or visits to special places, may help to clarify 'when'. Returning the child to the place where the abuse occurred may help establish which room was used, and more detail as to 'where').

What did the child wear as clothing? Did the child dress up in adult clothing or use make-up?

How did the perpetrator gain the child's co-operation? What was the coercion or bribe?

Who was the perpetrator? If he was a relative or friend of the child, the child may be able to provide the adult's second name or other confirmatory identification. This is especially important, if the child says "Mummy" or "Daddy", in families where there is more than one person who is a parental figure for the child. If he was a stranger, the presence of identifying features such as a moustache, beard, or glasses should be enquired about. Young children can be helped in this by drawing the perpetrator and adding such detail.

Were there any other people present? Were there any other children involved? Did any other adults 'help' the perpetrator? Did anyone else ever do something like that to the child? Where were non-involved family members (parents or siblings) and what did they do?

Was there any blood present on the child's body? Did the perpetrator ejaculate?

Did the child or the adult(s) use any substances (i.e. alcohol or drugs), and if so, what? Sometimes children can draw the tablet that they were made to ingest in great detail, including the manufacturer's trademark.

Did the perpetrator involve the child in the production of pornography? Was the child shown pornographic material?

Did the perpetrator involve the child in acts of bestiality or sadistic ritual, or use sexual aids?

After the initial interview, the extent of the victim's participation in the abusive contacts will need to be explored. This is an important factor in the child's psychological adaptation after disclosure. It is threatening to belabour this point during the first interview, as the child may already feel ashamed, guilty, or responsible for the abuse. Such psychological effects of victimisation will not necessarily be explored in an investigatory interview, but more likely in the ensuing evaluations for treatment.

The child may not spontaneously discuss any of these specific areas, yet the information is necessary to determine the child's immediate safety in the home, or to make visitation arrangements. The answer to some of these

questions will help guide whether to interview siblings who may have viewed the abuse or been privy to its existence.

6. *The closing phase*

As the interview comes to an end, the child needs reassurance and validation of the importance of the session. Direct congratulation is not appropriate, but to review briefly with the child what he has talked about is in order. If the child has struggled to overcome guilty feelings, this should be acknowledged. One of the most important messages to convey is that the interviewer appreciates and recognises the emotional feeling and struggle that the child has been through during the whole process. This validation of feeling is probably more important than 'pat' phrases such as, "It's not your fault".

The interviewer must prepare the child for what to expect in the future – continued interviews, psychological or developmental evaluation, possible treatment, etc. Predicting too far into the future should be avoided, however, and the interviewer should restrict him- or herself to describing the next step. The future course of events cannot always be predicted and may only instil fear in the child instead of allaying anxiety.

The overall investigation/evaluation process can be discussed with the child, possibly eliminating some of the powerless feelings that he or she may have. Again, honesty and openness are the guiding principles here, and if one does not expect to see the child again, that must be directly explained to him before the end of the interview.

Children of different ages

We have made reference to children of different ages throughout the above, but we mention some points relevant to specific age-groups here, in order to indicate areas that we feel require emphasis.

The younger child (up to age 7)

The pre-school or young school-age child's speech and language development is immature, and non-verbal techniques will need to be stressed. Too many words will confuse the pre-school-age child, especially when he is asked to draw similarities, state differences between persons or events, or to sequence events in a linear time frame. With pre-school children, words such as 'tickle' or 'playing games' may be used instead of 'touch'. This is because, for very young children, the abuse may be confusing and seen as a game by them. Furthermore, phrases such as "hurt you", or "do bad things to you" should be avoided. Many children do not perceive sexual abuse in such a way and consequently will be confused by such notions. With the younger child, the recommended questions outlined when inquiring about sexual abuse cannot be asked out of the blue. Interviewer and child will need to develop an understanding between them as to what it is that is being addressed, so that the questions asked are not too complex for the child. There are various ways to do this by using the child's own lead and interest. Some methods are discussed in more detail (see *Use of toys and play materials* above). We often use drawings to enable the child: 1. to know that we are talking about body parts; and 2. to identify and name those parts. After this has been established, simple inquiry about sexual abuse can be made. Established books can be used for this purpose; e.g. *Red Flag/Green Flag People, Anatomical Drawings* (see Appendix B). One can also use children's anatomy and physiology books, e.g. *The Body Book* (Appendix B). Alternatively, a body outline may be sketched on a piece of paper or on a blackboard and the child may join in the drawing. Occasionally, children will point to their own bodies. If this does happen, the child should be diverted from his own body to a drawing or doll figure in order to disclose further detail about sexual abuse. Similarly, dolls, whether anatomically correct or not, as well as other material such as clay, can be used to enable young children to focus upon the question of sexual abuse.

Pre-verbal children present even greater obstacles. The observation of free play then achieves greater significance, but great care must be taken not to overinterpret play. Children at age 1½–2½ years can sometimes respond to "Did X hurt you?" followed by demonstration on a doll or line drawing in response to "show me" (for an example, see Fig. 4). Additional parallel information from family and medical information may provide sufficient evidence of sexual abuse to warrant protection of the child. However, cases involving pre-verbal and barely verbal children are hard to substantiate at the present time. Unfortunately, paedophiles know this, and some choose young or handicapped children in order to avoid capture.

The primary-school-aged child (approximately aged 7–12)

During this age span, the starting stage is of special importance. This may be combined with a general assessment of mental status and psychological adjustment. During the course of the interview, time may be spent discussing the child's feelings, and the consequences of possible disclosure. This will often be necessary before the child will feel confident enough to entrust the interviewer with his or her secret. Art and drawing methods may be used during facilitation, but rarely anatomically correct dolls with this age group. 'Older' dolls, in male and female format, may be quite useful with this age group, as may anatomical drawings such as those by Groth (Appendix B).

Teenagers

With this age group, the question of the gender of the interviewer may be more important than with younger children. Once again, questions of privacy and the consequences of disclosure, as well as the confidentiality issues may well need to be discussed with the youngster before he or she will feel comfortable discussing the sexual abuse. In general, the style of the interview with a teenager consists of using talking methods rather than play. Care should be taken to limit and control gaze fixation with teenagers to lessen the sense of intrusion and embarrassment that they frequently experience. Interviewer style becomes very important with this age group; confidence, acceptance, and a lack of embarrassment being important aspects. With a teenager, it should be recognised that he or she may well have developed a collusive partnership with an abuser over a long period of repeated abuse ('accommodation', see Summit, 1983). Hence the need for great care with the questions and an acceptance of the teenager as a potentially complex victim. Similarly, the teenager, by this stage, may have abused other siblings or children in his or her care. The teenager will frequently resist the 'authority' of the interviewer, both because of his or her developmental stage and also possibly because of long-term intrafamilial abuse creating additional issues concerning authority. This may pose special problems during the interview, leading to the teenager asking the interviewer to justify why they **should** talk about it. In these circumstances the notion of 'should' is discouraged and the interviewer talks plainly and openly with the youngster about his or her predicament, the choices they face, and recommendations for the best way out of the current predicament.

The interview in context

The interview as described is part of a wider evaluation of a potential case. Further examination of the child may be necessary; paediatric assessment (Kolvin *et al*, 1988; Krugman & Jones, 1987; Hobbs & Wynne, 1987), general psychological and psychiatric assessment (Cox & Rutter, 1985; Hill, 1985); the child's parents will need to be seen and probably assessed (Jones *et al*, 1988; Kolvin *et al*, 1988). These assessments are not described in this book. After all these stages have been gone through, findings are interpreted, and finally conclusions can be drawn (see chapter 5).

5 The process of validation

Once the child's story has been elicited using the interviewing techniques outlined above, the clinician or police officer has to decide if it is a truthful account. This process in itself may be one for a court of law to make its own decision, based on the evidence, but nevertheless, the clinician will have to make his own decision. There is no ultimate test of truthfulness, and it is well-known that physiological measures of truth (such as the polygraph examination) are not 100% reliable. One is, therefore, left with an approach to validation that must add together the many factors connected with the allegation in order to say whether a particular child has or has not been sexually abused. Naturally, at each end of the spectrum will be those cases in which abuse clearly has or has not occurred, leaving a group of cases in between where the conclusion will be much more difficult. It is in this spirit that we provide a framework for considering whether a particular suspicion of sexual abuse is most likely to be true or untrue.

This approach to validation is based upon clinical experience of corroborated accounts, false ones, mistaken suspicions of CSA, and a review of the work of others (Benedek & Schetky, 1985; Faller, 1984; Goodwin et al, 1982; Green, 1986; Sgroi et al, 1982). One of us (DJ) has studied three case series of false reports that presented in separate contexts (Jones & McGraw, 1987; Jones & Seig, 1988). Additionally, there have been attempts to objectify the criteria which appear to be the most useful when attempting to verify an account of CSA (Undeutsch, 1982; Yuille, unpubl.). These are useful starting points, but definitive studies are not yet available. Hence, the approach set out below represents the items that have been found to be useful components of the clinical process of validation. They are not presented as definitive criteria for the assessment of the truthfulness of a report, but simply as a framework for making clinical decisions. The framework should represent the *degree of certainty* that can be applied to an individual case (Jones & McGraw, 1987; Jones & Seig, 1988; Kolvin et al, 1988).

Sgroi *et al* (1982) have described their approach to validation, emphasising that the process centres upon a knowledge of the dynamics of child sexual abuse, good interviewing skills, and an ability to interpret the behaviour and physical signs obtained from the investigative interviewing. They break down the process of validation into the assessment of the child's behaviour, the results of the interview with the child, an assessment of credibility, the physical indicators of child sexual abuse, and finally, the medical examination. Goodwin *et al* (1982) have similarly described their practice clinically, which lessens the likelihood that a false report may be adjudged true. Faller (1984) has considered the question of validation and emphasises the importance of observing an emotional response consistent with the nature of the abuse, the presence of any idiocyncratic memories surrounding the sexual incident itself, the importance of the child's viewpoint of the event, his statements to other children, his play, and his abnormal knowledge of sexuality itself, as helpful elements in the process.

The importance must be given to the child's statement itself as the primary source upon which to assess whether the allegation is true or not. All other information and findings may be considered as either supporting the child's statement, or alternatively detracting from its worth, but cannot substitute for the child's statement. It may be that in years to come there will be more concrete findings from techniques of physical examination or from physiological measures of truthfulness, but at the time of writing, these do not provide the certainty to make a definitive statement about whether the child is telling the truth or not. That assertion can only be based on the child's statement augmented by other observations and findings. Therefore, we shall first consider what aspects of the child's statement may give us helpful clues and leads as to veracity.

The child's statement

The statement is examined for explicit detail of an alleged sexual abuse. Younger children, particularly under the age of 5 years, are not able to relate as much detail as are older children (Goodman & Helgeson, 1985). However, the more detail that is recalled, the more likely it is that the account is truthful, especially as it is considered unlikely that an individual child can gain such detailed knowledge unless he had personal experience of the event in question.

The words and sentence formation should be congruent with the age and developmental status of the child; a 5-year-old child who falsely recanted her allegations, when asked why the sexual abuse had stopped some 18 months previously, said, "because it was inappropriate". This phrase belied its adult, rather than child origins. As time passes, children do adopt their therapist's and case-workers' language, and so may appear unbelievable for this reason. When this is a problem, reference to the early statements of the child can help establish veracity.

Unique or distinguishing detail should be sought. This may be found both within the account of the sexual encounter and/or in unrelated recollections.

Examples include children who describe smells and tastes associated with rectal, vaginal, or oral sex. One 4-year-old boy described a feeling of rectal stretching when being sodomised, ''I felt like I wanna' go pooh pooh''. Distinguishing detail may also be found in the description of the room or the clothes the child was wearing at the time. One 3-year-old girl said, ''I had my panties on backwards''.

The statement may be searched for evidence of a child's perspective of the abuse incident, in contrast to that of an adult or third-party.

The emotion expressed by the child during the interview is usually congruent with the events being described. A child may experience one part of the abuse as more offensive than another, but this differential may not coincide with the interviewer's assumption as to what was the worst experience for the child. We may further ask whether the child's account is given in a rehearsed or packaged manner, or with appropriate emotion. Is the allegation delivered at the slightest cue from the interviewer, or in one or two sentences without the usual difficulty and reserve or hesitancy that children show? Is the emotion expressed genuinely experienced, or is it hollow in its manner of expression? Is the child bland, unemotive, and seemingly little perturbed by serious exploitation. While we would not expect all of these features to be evident in a single account, their presence or absence can be helpful in assessing veracity. Clues as to the child's psychological response to the abusive incident should also be sought. Did the child feel sad, frightened, angry, or guilty? Did she describe a remote or removed state of mind (dissociation).

The pattern of the abuse described may help establish veracity, too. The clinical pattern in sexual abuse may not include intercourse, and may be restricted to oral or deviant sexual practices. In abuse by persons known to the child, it is common for there to be multiple incidents over time. A progression from fondling through oral sexual contact to intercourse over a period of months or years is common in incest cases.

The element of secrecy is usual and can be found in many accounts. ''This must be our special game – don't tell anyone, not even your mom''. Children may be coerced into activity, and/or threatened not to tell. They are frequently told that they will be physically harmed or removed from the people whom they love, if they do tell. Such coercion or threats are not always evident in the initial interviews if the child is too fearful.

There are other less-common features, which may help greatly to establish veracity. They include descriptions of pornographic involvement, sadism, and ritualism. These elements are probably underrecognised at present because we do not routinely inquire about them. Pornography may be present as part of the child's involvement in a sex ring (Burgess *et al*, 1984), or for consumption within the family only. One child described the ritual decapitation of a rabbit during her sexual abuse by a family friend, using the most graphic detail. The police were informed, searched the alleged perpetrator's basement, and discovered the dead animal, decapitated, just as the girl had described, along with other evidence of satanic ritual.

Supporting features

The factors considered below provide support, or alternatively, if inconsistent, may raise doubts as to the veracity of the child's statement. In those cases of abuse within the family, the biographies of other family members combined with the history of the family can provide helpful, supportive information. The alleged perpetrator's track record of violence, spouse abuse, alcohol and/or substance abuse, may indicate the type of individual who could be involved in sexual abuse of a child. Similarly, the non-involved parent's attitude and response to the allegation may be in keeping with the kind of responses often seen in child sexual-abuse cases. The family may have a prior history of neglecting and abusing children, and may have sexually abused other children in the past. The history of their parental attachment and involvement with their children may provide further clues. An assessment may be possible as to the degree of dysfunction in the family, providing further data that may support or detract from the statement the child has made.

The child's behaviour during the period when she was being sexually abused may show some of the features that show an association with child sexual abuse (see chapter 1). Whether the child being interviewed disclosed the abuse in a similar way to children in other confirmed cases should be considered. Who did she tell, and what motivated her to do so? Is the disclosure understandable, given the pressures normally existing on children not to tell? Answering these questions can provide helpful information that may support or detract from the child's statement.

The child may have made a statement to other people before this interview. Often children talk to other children, or perhaps to neighbours, babysitters, or teachers, and the contents of their statements to these people may usefully be compared with the statement obtained from interview. The question of consistency between different statements made by a single child is more complicated than appears at first glance. There is usually, in truthful accounts, a consistency of the core elements of the child's exploitation, but there may be some variation in the more peripheral aspects of the child's story. Thus, the question of consistency is not an all-or-nothing matter. It may vary with the degree of personal poignancy of the particular experience for that child. Similarly, as stated above, the more violent elements of coercion and threatening behaviour by the perpetrator may be very frightening for the child, and consequently these elements may be suppressed by the child for a longer period than the sexual aspects of the abuse. This may give an air of apparent inconsistency to a child's account of sexual abuse over a period of weeks or months, but running through the account will be a consistent thread. In contrast to this situation, false statements are made with monotonous consistency, and show no sign of variation over time.

The way in which the child uses toys, playthings and drawing materials may be revealing. His drawings may contain highly sexualised themes, and his play with dolls may show similar preoccupations. His knowledge of sexual anatomy and function is often asynchronous with that of children of a similar age and social background. Other children who were involved or were perhaps in the household at the same time may have a viewpoint concerning the sexual abuse of the child being interviewed. Sometimes, they may have actually seen the abuse occurring, or at least have some knowledge of the activity. Sometimes the child who is being abused may have shared their secret with a brother or sister. These supporting features may be considered in conjunction with the statement of the child, but cannot serve as a substitute for the child's statement.

Physical and physiological evidence

Gross physical evidence of sexual abuse only occurs in approximately 15% of all cases (Kerns, 1981). Descriptions of the physical abnormalities which clinicians have observed can be found in Hobbs & Wynne (1987), Kerns (1981), and Paul (1977, 1986). Cantwell (1983) has pointed to more subtle findings in sexually abused girls which may give an indication as to possible child sexual abuse. A search for evidence of ejaculation in vaginal, rectal, and oral orifices can provide further information (Krugman & Jones, 1987). The discovery of a potentially sexually transmitted disease may well confirm a suspicion of CSA (Neinstein *et al*, 1984). The use of the dye toluidine blue enhances the appearance of scar tissue in the perineal area and can be a useful aid to diagnosis (McCauley *et al*, 1986). There have been attempts to use microscopic techniques to show evidence of penetration, but at the present time there are not definitive studies with adequate control populations to be certain of the meaning of these early findings.

Physiological correlates of truthfulness – such as the polygraph examination – suffer again from the same lack of rigorous testing, and so, while they might provide an indication, cannot be used with confidence as a measure of truthfulness. Thus validation involves assessing as many of the above features as possible, in any single case, weighing the relative weight of the individual elements. The major emphasis should, however, be placed upon the child's statement itself.

Concluding remarks

Interviewing children who may have been sexually exploited requires a great deal from the professional in terms of a theoretical base and clinical knowledge. The application of these skills requires sensitivity to the needs of the individual child. For many children, successful application of these skills can mean relief from a veritable nightmare of misuse, thus beginning the slow process of repair and starting anew. It is our hope that if the initial interviews are conducted appropriately, the ensuing process will be more easily borne.

Appendix A

Suggested contents for an interviewing room

Necessary toys and play materia's

Standard baby doll or rag doll – 12-14 in – with crib (not anatomically correct)
Doll's clothes
Dolls suitable for elementary-school-aged children
Small dolls' house and furniture
Set of small doll figures – 3 in – including family set, doctor-and-nurse set, police, and fire sets, (last three are useful but not essential)
Open play car
Art materials: white paper, felt-tip pens, crayons, Play do®, or clay

Additional materials

Second dolls' house (useful for custody evaluations, foster-care placement, etc.)
Set of anatomically correct dolls
Plasticine-shaping tools and board
Toy telephones (two)
Police and/or ambulance play car
Tape recorder (audio)
Toy soldiers
Zoo animals
Puppets (set of humans – black and white)
Family face puppets
Animal puppets – glove variety
Picture books graded towards children of various ages including pictures of anatomy and body functions
'Red Flag/Green Flag' book (Appendix B).
Anatomical drawings (Appendix B).

Dressing–undressing puzzle by Galt Toys
The children's clothing are the puzzle pieces that lift out to show a nude boy and girl. The inlaid, wooden tray is brightly painted in non-toxic colours. 9½ × 12 in, 14 pieces.

Deluxe dolls' house family
Plastic, articulated figures with moveable head, arms, and legs. Their knees also bend, so the dolls may sit. These dolls are available from Fisher Price, only in the USA.

Most of these items are obtainable through local toy shops. Special resources to aid the interviewer are listed in Appendix B. Mail-order catalogues of educational toys are available:

> Early Learning Centre,
> Hawksworth,
> Swindon, SN2 1TT
> (0793) 610171
>
> Hestair Hope Ltd,
> St Philips Drive,
> Royton,
> Oldham, OL8 6AG
> (061) 633-3935

Appendix B

Resources for the interviewer

Books

Red Flag/Green Flag People (1986) by Rape and Abuse Crisis Center of Fargo-Moorhead, illustrated by Kecia Softing Freed. This is a colouring book that talks about touch by different people in different ways. It identifies touch that feels good as 'green', and touch that feels scary, confusing, or bad as 'red'. Children are asked to identify good and bad touches by colouring the flags below each picture. There is also a page which asks the child to colour areas with red if they were touched in an unpleasant manner. The book is available from:

> Rape and Abuse Center of Fargo-Moorhead
> P.O. Box 2984
> Fargo, ND 58108
> USA
> (701) 293-7298

The Body Book (1979) by Claire Rayner. London: Pan Books.
This book describes the anatomy and physiology of the human body in a way which is understandable by children 4 years and upwards. There are good line illustrations.

Anatomical Drawings by A. Nicholas Groth, illustrated by Thomas M. Stevenson, Jr. This is a collection of line drawings of naked children, adolescents and adults of different races for use in the investigation and management of child sexual abuse. It is available from:

> Forensic Mental Health Associates, Inc.,
> 3 Ireland Road,
> Newtown Center, MA 02159,
> USA
> (617) 332-0228

Anatomically correct dolls

The following are suppliers of anatomically correct dolls:

> Musha Dolls (made to order)
> Jean Towe,
> 37a Twyford,
> Banbury OX17 3JQ
> (0295) 810551
>
> Show and Tell Dolls
> 23 Marley Comb Road,
> Camelsdale,
> Haslemere,
> Surrey GU27 3SN
> (0428) 53987

National resource organisations

The following organisations provide information on audio-visual aids and other training materials that are available for professionals. Some of them also have bibliographies and lists available on request.

National Society for the Prevention of Cruelty to Children (NSPCC)

The NSPCC has a network of child-protection teams offering services to abused children and their families in England, Wales, and Northern Ireland. At both national and local levels, the society offers a consultancy service to professionals, and provides multidisciplinary training. The Headley Library, at Saffron Hill, is a major resource centre bringing together a wide range of materials on child abuse. It can be used for reference in person, or for loans by prior arrangement. The Society's publication list is available on request. Please send a large SAE to:

> 67 Saffron Hill,
> London EC1N 8RS
> (01) 242-1626

Training Advisory Group on the Sexual Abuse of Children (TAGOSAC)

TAGOSAC produce a training materials resource list which includes audio-visual materials. Please send a large SAE to:

The TAGOSAC CSA Project,
at the National Children's Bureau,
8 Wakley Street,
London EC1V 7QE
(01) 278-9441 ext. 272

Standing Committee on Sexually Abused Children (SCOSAC)

SCOSAC produce an information pack which is available at a cost of £3. Please request the one for professionals. SCOSAC also produce a list of video-tapes available in the UK, as well as other information broadsheets. They have a library of approximately 100 books and 200 articles that can be referenced in person by prior arrangement. They are housed at:

SCOSAC,
2nd floor, Crown House,
London Road,
Morden,
Surrey SM4 5DX
(01) 545-3428/9

British Association for the Study and Prevention of Child Abuse and Neglect (BASPCAN)

BASPCAN is a multidisciplinary professional organisation, which publishes *Child Abuse Review*, three times a year. The review may be obtained on application to the address below:

Dr Malcolm Brown,
Membership Secretary,
3 Parkstone Close,
Hastings Hill,
Sunderland,
Tyne and Wear SR4 5PA

References

ALLPORT, G. W. & POSTMAN, L. (1947) *The Psychology of Rumor*. New York: Henry Holt.

AMERICAN PSYCHIATRIC ASSOCIATION (1980) *Diagnostic and Statistical Manual of Mental Disorder* (3rd edn) (DSM–III). Washington, DC: American Psychiatric Association.

BECKER, J. V. & ABEL, G. G. (1984) *Methodological and Ethical Issues Evaluating and Treating Adolescent Sexual Offenders*. Bethesda, MA: NIMH.

BENEDEK, E. P., & SCHETKY, D. H. (1985) Allegations of sexual abuse in child custody and visitation disputes. In *Emerging Issues in Child Psychiatry and the Law* (eds D. H. Schetky & E. B. Benedek). New York: Brunner/Mazel.

BERLINER, L. & BARBIERI, M. K. (1984) The testimony of the child victim of sexual assault. *Journal of Social Issues*, **40**, 125–137.

BROSS, D. C., KRUGMAN, R. D., LENHERR, M., ROSENBERG, D. & SCHMIDT, B. D. (eds) (1988) *The New Child Protection Team Handbook*. New York: Garland Press.

BROWN, A. L., BRANSFORD, J. D., FERRARA, R. A. & CAMPIONE, J. C. (1983) Learning, remembering and understanding. In *Handbook of Child Psychology* (eds J. H. Flavell & E. M. Maskman), pp. 77–166. New York: Wiley.

BROWNE, A. & FINKELHOR, D. (1986) Initial and long-term effects: A review of the research. In *A Sourcebook on Child Sexual Abuse* (ed. D. Finkelhor) Beverley Hills: Sage.

BURGESS, A. & HOLMSTROM, L. L. (1975) Rape trauma syndrome. *American Journal of Psychiatry*, **131**, 981–986.

—— HARTMAN, C. R., MCCAUSLAND, M. P. & POWERS, P. (1984) Response patterns in children and adolescents exploited through sex rings and pornography. *American Journal of Psychiatry*, **141**, 656–662.

—— & HOLMSTROM, L. L. (1975) Sexual trauma of children and adolescents: sex, pressure and secrecy. *Nursing Clinics of North America*, **101**, 551–563.

BUTLER-SLOSS, E. (1988) *Report of the Inquiry into Child Abuse in Cleveland in 1987*. London: HMSO.

CANTWELL, H. (1983) Vaginal inspection as it relates to young girls. *Child Abuse and Neglect*, **7**, 171–176.

CECI, S. J., ROSS, D. & TOGLIA, M. (1987a) Age differences in suggestibility: narrowing the uncertainties. In *Children's Eye-witness Memory* (eds S. Ceci, M. P. Toglia & D. Ross). New York: Springer–Verlag.

——, TOGLIA, M. P. & ROSS, D. (1987b) *Children's Eye-witness Memory*. New York: Springer–Verlag.

COLE, C. B. & LOFTUS, E. F. (1987) The memory of children. In *Children's Eye-witness Memory* (eds S. Ceci, M. P. Toglia & D. Ross). New York: Springer–Verlag.

CONTE, J. R., BERLINER, L. & SCHUERMANN, J. R. (1987) *The Impact Of Sexual Abuse On Children: Final Technical Report* Bethesda, Maryland: National Institute For Mental Health.

—— & —— (1988) The Impact of Sexual Abuse on Children: Clinical Findings. In *Handbook on Sexual Abuse of Children: Assessment and Treatment Issues* (ed. L. Walker). New York: Springer.

COX, A. & RUTTER, M. (1985) Diagnostic appraisal and interviewing. In *Child and Adolescent Psychiatry, Modern Approaches* (eds M. Rutter & L. Hersov). London: Blackwell.

DALE, P. S., LOFTUS, E. F. & RATHBUN, L. (1978) The influence of the form of the question on the eyewitness testimony of preschool children. *Journal of Psycholinguistic Research*, **7**, 269–277.

DAVIES, G., STEPHENSON-ROBB, Y. & FLINN, R. (1986) The reliability of children's testimony. *International Legal Practitioner*, 95–103.

DENT, H. R. (1982) The effects of interviewing strategies on the results of interviews with child witnesses. In *Reconstructing the Past: The Role of Psychologists in Criminal Trials* (ed. A. Trankell). Stockholm: Norstedt.

—— & STEPHENSON, G. M. (1979) An experimental study of the effectiveness of different techniques of questioning child witnesses. *British Journal of Social and Clinical Psychology*, **18**, 41–51.

DEPARTMENT OF HEALTH AND SOCIAL SECURITY (1988) *Working Together*. London: HMSO.

DONALDSON, M. (1978) *Children's Minds*. Glasgow: Fontana.

EVERSTINE, D. S. & EVERSTINE, L. (1983) The adult woman victim of rape. In *People in Crisis: Strategic Therapeutic Interventions* (eds D. S. Everstine & L. Everstine). New York: Brunner Mazel.

FALLER, K. C. (1984) Is the child victim of sexual abuse telling the truth? *Child Abuse and Neglect*, **8**, 473–481.

FINKELHOR, D. (1979) *Sexually Victimized Children*. New York: Free Press.

—— (1984) Four preconditions of sexual abuse: A model. In *Child Sexual Abuse; New Theory and Research* (ed. D. Finkelhor). New York: Free Press.

FRASER, B. G. (1981) Sexual child abuse: legislation and law in the United States. In *Sexual Abused Children and Their Families* (eds P. B. Mrazek & C. H. Kempe). Oxford: Pergamon.

GARVEY, C. (1977) *Play*. Cambridge, MA: Harvard University Press. (The Developing Child Series).

GELINAS, D. J. (1983) The persisting negative effects of incest. *Psychiatry*, **46**, 312–332.

GELMAN, R. (1978) Cognitive development. *Annual Review of Psychology*, **29**, 297–332.

GIARRETTO, H. (1976) Humanistic treatment of father–daughter incest. In *Child Abuse and Neglect: The Family and the Community* (eds R. E. Helfer & C. H. Kempe), pp. 143–168. Cambridge, MA: Ballinger.

GOODMAN, G. S. (1984) The child witness: conclusions and future directions for research and legal practice. *Journal of Social Issues*, **40**, 157–175.

—— & JONES, D. P. H. (1988) The emotional effects of criminal court testimony on child sexual assault victims: a preliminary report. In *The Child Witness: Do the Courts Abuse Children* (ed. G. Davies & J. Drinkwater). Leicester: British Psychological Society. *Issues in Criminological and Legal Psychology*, no. **13**.

—— & HELGESON, V. S. (1985) Child sexual assault: Children's memory and the law. *University of Miami Law Review*, **40**, 181–208.

GOODWIN, J. (1982) The use of drawings in incest cases. In *Sexual Abuse: Incest Victims and Their Families* (ed. J. Goodwin), pp. 47–56. London: John Wright.

——, SAHD, D. & RADA, R. T. (1982) False accusations and false denials of incest: Clinical myths and clinical realities. In *Sexual Abuse: Incest Victims and Their Families* (ed. J. Goodwin), pp. 17–26. London: John Wright.

GREEN, A. H. (1986) True and false allegations of sexual abuse in child custody disputes. *Journal of the American Academy of Child Psychiatry*, **25**, 449–456.

GUDJONSSON, G. H. & GUNN, J. (1982) The competence and reliability of a witness in a criminal court: A case report. *British Journal of Psychiatry*, **41**, 624–627.

HALEY, J. (1973) *Uncommon Therapy: The Psychiatric Techniques of Milton Erickson*. New York: Norton.

HELFER, R. & KEMPE, R. (eds) (1987) *The Battered Child* (4th edn). Chicago: The University of Chicago Press.

HILL, P. (1985) The diagnostic interview with the individual child. In *Child and Adolescent Psychiatry, Modern Approaches* (eds M. Rutter & L. Hersov). London: Blackwell.

HOBBS, C. J. & WYNNE, J. M. (1987) Management of sexual abuse. *Archives of Diseases in Childhood*, **62**, 1182–1187

JAMES, J. & MEYERDING, J. (1977) Early sexual experience and prostitution. *American Journal of Psychiatry*, **134**, 1381–1385.

JAMPOLE, L. & WEBER, M. K. (1987) An assessment of the behavior of sexually abused and non-sexually abused children with anatomically correct dolls. *Child Abuse and Neglect*, **11**, 187–192.

JOHNSON, M. K. & FOLEY, M. A. (1984) Differentiating fact from fantasy: The reliability of children's memory. *Journal of Social Issues*, **40**, 33–50.

JONES, D. P. H. & KRUGMAN, R. (1986) Can a three-year-old child bear witness to her sexual assault and attempted murder? *Child Abuse and Neglect*, **10**, 253–258.

——, KEMPE, R. S. & STEELE, B. F. (1988) The psychiatric evaluation and treatment plan. In *The New Child Protection Team Handbook* (eds D. Bross *et al*). New York: Garland.

—— & MCGRAW, J. M. (1987) Reliable and fictitious accounts of sexual abuse to children. *Journal of Interpersonal Violence*, **2**, 27–45.

—— & SEIG, A. (1988) Child sexual abuse allegations in custody or visitation disputes. In *Sexual Abuse Allegations in Custody and Visitation Disputes* (ed. B. Nicholson) Washington DC: American Bar Association.

KERNS, D. L. (1981) Medical assessment of child sexual abuse. In Mrazek P. B., Kempe, C. H. (eds) *Sexually Abused Children and Their Families* (eds P. B. Mrazek & C. H. Kempe), pp. 129–141. Oxford: Pergamon.

KING, M. A. & YUILLE, J. C. (1987) Suggestibility and the child witness. In *Children's Eyewitness Memory* (eds S. Ceci, M. P. Toglia & D. Ross). New York: Springer–Verlag.

KIRBY, R. & RADFORD, J. (1976) *Individual Differences*. London: Methuen.

KOLVIN, I., STEINER, H., BAMFORD, F. TAYLOR, M., WYNNE, J., JONES, D. & ZEITLIN, H. (1988) Child sexual abuse – some principles of good practice. *British Journal of Hospital Medicine*, **39**, 54–62.

KRUGMAN, R. & JONES, D. P. H. (1987) Incest and other forms of sexual abuse. In *The Battered Child* (eds R. S. Kempe & R. E. Helfer) London: University of Chicago Press.

LEVENTHAL, J. M., BENTOVIM, A., ELTON, A., TRANTER, M. & READ, L. (1987) What to ask when sexual abuse is suspected. *Archives of Disease in Childhood*, **62**, 1188–1195.

LINDBERG, M. (1980) Is knowledge base development a necessary and sufficient condition for memory development? *Journal of Experimental Child Psychology*, **30**, 401–410.

LISTER, E. D. (1982) Forced silence: A neglected dimension of trauma. *American Journal of Psychiatry*, **139**, 867–872.

LOFTUS, E. F. & DAVIES, G. M. (1984) Distortions in the memory of children. *Journal of Social Issues*, **40**, 51–67.

LUKIANOWICZ, N. (1972) Incest I – paternal incest; II – other types of incest. *British Journal of Psychiatry*, **120**, 301–313.

MACFARLANE, K. (1985) Diagnostic evaluations and the use of videotapes in child sexual abuse cases. *University Of Miami Law Review*. **40**, 135–165.

MARIN, B. V., HOLMES, D. L. GUTH, M. & KOVAC, P. (1979) The potential of children as eye witnesses. *Law and Human Behavior*, **3**, 295–306.

MCCAWLEY, J., GORMAN, R. L. & GUZINSKI, G. (1986) Toluidine blue in the detection of perineal lacerations in paediatric and adolescent sexual abuse victims. *Paediatrics*, **78**, 1039–1043.

MCGURK, H. (1975) *Growing and Changing*. London: Methuen.

MEHTA, M. N., LOKESHWAR, M. R. BHATT, S. C. ATHAVALE, V. B. & KALKARNI, B. S. (1979) Rape in children. *Child Abuse and Neglect*, **3**, 671–677.

MEISELMAN, K. C. (1978) *Incest: A Psychological Study of Causes and Effects with Treatment Recommendations*. San Francisco, Jossey Bass.

MELTON, G., BULKLEY, J. & WULKAR, D. (1981) Competency of children as witnesses. In *Child Sexual Abuse and the Law* (ed. J. Bulkley), pp. 125–145. Washington, DC: American Bar Association.

MOORE, J. & KENDALL, D. G. (1971) Children's concepts of reproduction. *Journal of Sex Research*, **7**, 42–61.

MRAZEK, P. B. (1981) Definition and recognition of sexual child abuse. In *Sexually Abused Children and Their Families* (ed. P. B. Mrazek & C. H. Kempe). Oxford: Pergamon Press.

—— KEMPE, C. H. (eds) (1981) *Sexually Abused Children and Their Families*. Oxford: Pergamon Press.

MUSSEN, P. H., CONGER, J. J., KAGAN, J. & HUSTON, A. C. (1984) *Child Development and Personality*. New York: Harper and Row.

NAITORE, C. E. (1982) Art therapy with sexually abused children. In *Handbook of Clinical Intervention in Child Sexual Abuse* (ed. S. M. Sgroi), pp. 269–308. Lexington, MA: D. C. Heath.

NEINSTEIN, L. S., GOLDENRING, J. & CARPENTER, S. (1984) Nonsexual transmission of sexually transmitted diseases: an infrequent occurrence. *Paediatrics,* **74**, 67–76.

OUNSTED, C. & LYNCH, M. (1976) Family pathology as seen in England. In *Child Abuse and Neglect: The Family and the Community* (eds R. E. Helfer & C. H. Kempe), pp. 75–86. Cambridge, MA: Ballinger.

OXFORDSHIRE JOINT CHILD PROTECTION COMMITTEE (1987) *Child Protection Procedures.* Oxford: Oxfordshire Social Services Department.

PAUL, D. M. (1977) The medical examination in sexual offences against children. *Medicine, Science and the Law,* **17**, 251–258.

—— (1986) What really did happen to baby Jane – The medical aspects of the investigation of alleged sexual abuse of children. *Medicine Science and the Law,* **26**, 85–102.

PERLMUTTER, M. (ed.) (1980) *Children's Memory. New Directions in Child Development,* no. **10**. San Francisco, CA: Jossey–Bass.

PETERSON, C. & SELIGMAN, M. E. P. (1983) Learned helplessness and victimization. *Journal of Social Issues,* **39**, 103–116.

PIZZEY, E. (1974) Scream quietly or the neighbours will hear. London: Penguin.

PORTER, F. S., BLICK, L. C. & SGROI, S. M. (1982) Treatment of the sexually abused child. In *Handbook of Clinical Intervention in Child Sexual Abuse* (ed. S. M. Sgroi), pp. 109–145. Lexington, MA: D. C. Heath.

PRICE, D. W. W. (1984) The development of children's comprehension of recurring episodes. Doctoral dissertation, University of Denver, CO.

PYNOOS, R. S. & ETH, S. (1984) The child as witness to homicide. *Journal of Social Issues,* **40**, 87–108.

ROSENBLATT, D. B. (1980) *Play.* In *Scientific Foundations of Developmental Psychiatry* (ed. M. Rutter). London: Heinemann.

ROSENFELD, A., BAILEY, R., SIEGEL, B. & BAILEY, G. (1986) Determining incestuous contact between parent and child: frequency of children touching parents' genitals in a non-clinical population. *Journal of the American Academy of Child Psychiatry,* **25**, 481–484.

RUBIN, K. H. FEIN, G. G. & VANDENBURY, B. (1983) *Play.* In *Handbook of Child Psychology* (ed. P. H. Mussen) vol. iv. Chichester: John Wiley.

RUSSELL, D. E. H. (1986) *The Secret Trauma: Incest in the Lives of Girls and Women.* New York: Basic Books.

RUTTER, M. (1980) Psychosexual development. In *Scientific Foundations of Developmental Psychiatry* (ed. M. Rutter). London: Heinemann.

—— (1985) Resilience in the face of adversity; protective factors and psychiatric disorder. *British Journal of Psychiatry,* **147**, 598–611.

SCHECTER, M. D. & ROBERGE, L. (1986) Sexual exploitation. In *Child Abuse and Neglect: The Family and the Community* (eds R. E. Helfer & C. H. Kempe). Cambridge, Massachusetts: Ballinger.

SGROI, M. (1982) *Handbook of Clinical Intervention in Child Sexual Abuse.* Lexington, MA: D. C. Heath.

——, PORTER, F. S. & BLICK, L. C. (1982) Validation of child sexual abuse. In *Handbook of Clinical Intervention in Child Sexual Abuse* (ed. S. M. Sgroi), pp. 39–79. Lexington, MA: D. C. Heath.

SHENGOLD, L. (1967) The effects of overstimulation: rat people. *International Journal of Psychoanalysis,* **48**, 403–415.

SIMPSON, C. A., & PORTER, G. L. (1981) Self-mutilation in children and adolescents. *Bulletin of the Meninger Clinic,* **45**, 428–438.

STEMBER, C. J. (1980) Art therapy: A new use in the diagnosis and treatment of sexually abused children. In *Sexual Abuse of Children: Selected Readings.* Washington, DC: US. Department of Health and Human Services.

SUMMIT, R. (1983) The child sexual abuse accommodation syndrome. *Child Abuse and Neglect,* **7**, 177–193.

TAYLOR, D. C. (1982) The components of sickness: diseases, illnesses and predicaments. In *One Child* (eds J. Apley & C. Ounsted) pp. 1–13. London: Heinemann.

TERR, L. (1979) Children of Chowchilla: Study of psychic trauma. *Psychoanalytic Study of the Child*, **34**, 547–623.

TIZARD, B. & HARVEY, D. (1977) *The Biology of Play*. London: Heinemann, SIMP.

TODD, C. M. & PERLMUTTER, M. (1980) Reality recalled by preschool children. In *Children's Memory: New Directions in Child Development*, no. **10**, 69–85. San Francisco, CA: Jossey–Bass.

TULLY, B. & CAHILL, D. (1984) *Police Interviewing of the Mentally Handicapped*. London: Police Foundation.

TYLER, A. H. & BRASSARD, M. R. (1984) Abuse in the investigation and treatment of intrafamilial child sexual abuse. *Child Abuse and Neglect*, **81**, 47–53.

UNDEUTSCH, V. (1982) Statement reality analysis. In *Reconstructing the Past: The Role of Psychologists in Criminal Trials* (ed. A. Trankell), pp. 27–56. Stockholm: P. A. Norsted & Sons.

VIZARD, E., BENTOVIM, A. & TRANTER, M. (1987) Interviewing sexually abused children. *Adoption and Fostering*, **11**, 20–25.

WATERMAN, J. (1986) Developmental considerations. In *Sexual Abuse of Young Children* (ed. K. MacFarlane *et al*). London: Guilford Press.

WHITE, S., STROM, G. A., SANTILLI, G. & HALPIN, B. M. (1986) Interviewing young sexual abuse victims with anatomically correct dolls. *Child Abuse and Neglect*, **10**, 519–529.

WINNICOTT, D. W. (1971) *Therapeutic Consultations in Child Psychiatry*. London: Hogarth Press.

ZARAGOZA, M. S. (1987) Memory suggestibility and eye-witness testimony in children and adults. In *Children's Eye-witness Memory* (eds S. Ceci, M. P. Toglia & D. Ross). New York: Springer–Verlag.